The Boomer Generation

the tantalising tale of a boom that went bust

Carole McCall is a former Civil Servant and Business Woman who has worked as a Life Coach, NLP Trainer, Psychotherapist and Hypnotherapist for many years. Working in the United Kingdom, Ireland, Spain and America, she has helped many people to solve their own problems. This book is a story of the glamorous boom years that she hoped would last forever and the difficult busted years that she thought would never end. She is a grandmother of seven small children and lives in Tunbridge Wells with her husband and a small white Bichon Fris called Stella. *The Boomer Generation* is the tantalising tale of a boom that went bust.

By the same Author –

The Fourth Generation

The Lotus Generation

The Boomer Generation

the tantalising tale of a boom that went bust

Carole McCall

Arena Books

First published in 2015 by Arena Books

Arena Books
6 Southgate Green
Bury St. Edmunds
IP33 2BL

www.arenabooks.co.uk

Distributed in America by Ingram International, One Ingram Blvd., PO Box
3006, La Vergne, TN 37086-1985, USA.

Carole McCall
    The Boomer Generation *the tantalising tale of a boom that went bust*

British Library cataloguing in Publication Data. A catalogue record for this Book is
available from the British Library.

ISBN-13 978-1-909421-51-6

BIC classifications:- BTP, BGB, BGXA, WBA, WTL, WTM.

Printed and bound by Lightning Source UK

Cover design

by Jason Anscomb

Typeset in
Times New Roman

Dedicated

to my

Wonderful Children

Glossary of leading persons featured in this book and their relationship with the author

Mona - mother

Hester - grandmother.

Hannah - great grandmother.

Miranda - daughter.

Alexandra - paternal grandmother

Gillian - sister

Suzanne and Emma - daughters-in-law

Grant - husband

Theo and James - sons

Alistair - son-in-law

Harry - brother

Murray - father

Malcolm - brother-in-law

The Baby Boomers are typically regarded as those people born between the mid nineteen forties and the mid nineteen sixties

CONTENTS

PREFACE   13

Part I

1 - The rain is pattering on the roof   17
2 - How did I end up here?   18
3 - I think we are beginning to settle here   22
4 - Life in another place   25
5 - "Mum, I just saw Father Christmas"   28
6 - My Grandmother Alexandra   30
7 - What Grandmother Alexandra did next?   32
8 - Happy Heidelberg adventure   34
9 - Can you see that Schloss?   38
10 – I am going back to work   41
11 – Dubrovnik is a lovely place   45
12 – A lovely evening   47
13 – The scent of lavender   50
14 – Things that go bump in the night   51
15 – Dawn is breaking over there   54
16 – Please don't make me do this again   58
17 – What have I done this time?   61
18 – The quivering omelette   64
19 – The wild flower posy   67
20 – If I am injured do not send for my sister   68
21 – I love this lake   71
22 – Have we sold our house?   72
23 – They have rifled my knickers drawer   74
24 – I need to start my own life Mum   76
25 – Is that a truck we are following?   78
26 – The big bear hug   81
27 – Wherever is my elan?   82
28 – Please don't go to work today   85
29 – Self-indulgence is the name of his game   88
30 – I need to get my head together   92
31 – We need to pull together   94
32 – The money mail stand   95
33 – My difficult day   96
34 – Why can't we all go?   98
35 – What is going on here?   101
36 – I have finally found you   104
37 – She should know   105
38 – Up and down the country   108

39 – A trip to Harley street   110
40 – The dratted egg salad   112
41 – Who ever is making that noise?   114
42 – The days went by in a haze   115
43 – I am off to Oxfam   116
44 – I have cheekbones   118
45 – A lifetime wardrobe   119
46 – The rose perfume incident   120
47 – The dress parade   122
48 – A ticket outside Oxfam   124
49 – Who is driving the car?   125

Part II

50 – A night out with Margaret Rutherford   126
51 – The impacted wisdom teeth   128
52 – The Morris dancers   129
53 – The Pirates of Penzance   130
54 – A holiday for twenty people   131
55 – The football team is in the lift   133
56 – How nice to see you   136
57 – Father's big birthday   138
58 – Time for a change in my life   140
59 – A historical snooze   142
60 – This is a good year for us all   144
61 – We are alone at last   146
62 – It always rains in the Lake District   148
63 – The Summer season   151
64 – Horse racing and all that   153
65 – Our lovely weekend away   155
66 – Who's that ringing the bell?   156
67 – The Summer of the party   158
68 – The centre of the crowd   160
69 – I do not like the ambience here   161
70 – Lynne   163
71 – Anne   165
72 – Jessica   167
73 – Up town girl   168
74 – The VAT inspector   170
75 – The Gothic house   172
76 – What about a girls' holiday   175
77 – The French and the Americans   177
78 – The foundation garment   179

79 – Carmen Miranda's hat   181
80 – A perfect days in August   183
81 – The forsaken Mantilla   185
82 – The play at the Savoy   187
83 – The dogs are still asleep   188
84 – Home again, home again   189
85 – A chronic insomnia   192
86 – The bed under the window   194
87 – The hour of the Wolf   195
88 – The Cinderella hour   197

Part III

89 – She occasionally flaps her wings   199
90 – The expensive face cream   202
91 – The book collector   203
92 – My Mother's dress-making skills   204
93 – The What was wrong list   207
94 – Bright and early   208
95 – Two weeks of fun   211
96 – I love this place   212
97 – Home again, home again   214
98 – A political family   216
99 – A political change   219
100-The engagement in Paris   220
101-Lilies and Mantovani   221
102-Do you remember where you were?   223
103-The Prime Minister and the Queen   224
104-Christmas lunch is for twenty this year   225
105-Laura and her sisters   226
106-Are you a famous pop group?   229
107-Finding the right outfit   230
108-The baking paraphernalia   232
109-The night before the Wedding   235
110-The morning of the Wedding   237

Recipes for our travels   241

Preface

You are a child of the universe, no less than the trees and the stars; you have a right to be here. And whether or not it is clear to you, no doubt the universe is unfolding as it should.
Max Ehrmann, *Desiderata*

The Baby Boomer Generation had everything including freedom, music, power and enough excitement to power a fleet of rocket ships. Easy access to the professions, inexpensive housing and a voice to be heard all came with the territory.

That sense of eternal sunshine that made everything glow and gleam, seemed like an everlasting reality. We did not think twice as we chased the mirage of unattainable possibility.

There was a certain kind of post-war woman that was raised in the suffocating fifties fairyland and in a society that told her there was absolutely only one man in the world for her. A handsome, reliable and responsible man was going to love her forever in a beautiful cottage with roses around the door.

This woman was a teenager in the sixties who could not believe her luck at being invited to this vibrant life party: where everybody danced in miniskirts all night long to the beat of music nobody had ever heard before.

She was a young mother in the seventies who lived the vegetable growing, bread-making good life and then rushed back to work because she had read about feminism and that seductive philosophy had turned the dial on her fuzzy self-image and made it clear and sharp.

She was a loving but determined parent and conscientious employee in the eighties. She was an excellent hostess for her husband when he needed her and a part of every parent teacher association and school governing body that would have her.

Did I also mention that she was slender and glamorous with a beautiful garden and always wore perfume?

Her name was Gullible; her name was Me……

In the second decade of the new millennium it is hard to imagine a time when I did not know the rules that seems so simple now.

How was I ever so naive inside whilst presenting such an articulate and capable front to the outside world?

As I airily made my family's life choices, which included moving us around with my husband's job, I really was not aware of the following salient facts:

a) House prices can go crashing down as well as sailing upwards.

b) Moving house with small children is a breeze but you always move teenagers at your peril.

c) Just because the main breadwinner has a senior position with a blue chip company today, there is no guarantee he will have one tomorrow.

d) His version of love and commitment may not be yours. You cannot read his mind and he has absolutely no idea what's going on in yours.

e) You may think your husband is the exception to the rule, he isn't. As much as you love him, he is just a man. He really is just man.......

f)Just because your precious children tell you their new house, their new school, that new friend is fine does not mean they are not going to tell you something entirely different years later and with enough rancour to pierce and occasionally shatter your fragile heart.

g) A happy home can put its arms around one unhappy member. However if every single member of the family is hurting because their life has changed, you get to live in an unhappy home no matter how hard you try.

h) You have to learn to say *No* out loud .You cannot always say *Yes* as it always has consequences, even if it is just for your peace of mind. Practice rolling the word *No* round your mouth in front of the mirror just to see how it feels. You should never have to make a decision quickly, if you are forced to make one without time for reflection then the answer should always be *No*.

i) You matter too, particularly your financial security. Do not ever forget that fact even if you forget everything else you ever learn. Repeat after me.....*you matter too*.

j) One day you are going to be a lot older than you are now. You will still be the person that you are today, except it will be harder to get out of the chair without a little moan escaping from your lips. It will also be much harder to apply eyeliner on your ever so slightly crinkled eyelids!

k). It is always best to plan for a rainy day because that particular occasion is riding across the sky now, on a fluffy white cumulus congestus cloud, with your name written right across it in letters a mile high.

l) You are not a victim no matter how terrible you feel today, as what goes down must come up again eventually!

Whilst my children were small I had already moved the family three times with my husband and his career. These moves had gone well with lots of planning and foresight.

We were living in a lovely five bedroomed home in a Lakeland town. I had a great job which allowed me to work flexi time so I was always around for the children.

I also miraculously occasionally got to go to concerts and dancing with my friends and to the theatre with my husband.

My parents and siblings lived within a three mile radius and we were all very supportive of each other. In short we all loved our lives but my husband wanted to take this promotion three hundred and fifty miles away and as he explained "it would mean a better life for us".

This particular time we were moving away from our lives when my precious children were in their early teens and they were leaving their extended family, friends and schools behind.

In an exquisite state of naivety and determination I took a giant leap into the unknown, dragging my unsuspecting teenagers behind me. In one fell swoop my life became a cliché.

Let's examine what a cliché is. It's a phrase or opinion that is overused and betrays lack of original thought or a trite expression, often a figure of speech whose effectiveness has been worn out through overuse and excessive familiarity.

 a) Opposites attract.

 b) Scared out of my wits.

c) All is fair in love and war.

d) All's well that ends well.

e) Every cloud has a silver lining.

f) Time heals all wounds.

A cliché could be a middle age man running off with his secretary, buying a sports car, throwing caution to the winds as he pursues his own goals.

How can it be a cliché if it's your life?

Nobody has ever felt pain like you feel when it's you that is experiencing redundancy, your husband that has run off, it's you who is losing your house.

We are not clichés we are living breathing human beings and we are allowed to feel what we feel.

This is the story of my journey from excitement to despair and back to reality again. How I accepted a husband who was not obeying even one of the rules, because I was obeying all of the rules including the one that stated that marriage is for life.

I did not know who had laid these rules down I only knew catastrophe would befall me if I did not accept my situation and get on with it…Whatever it was.

Leo Tolstoy made perfect sense when he wrote "Outer consequences are not in our power to control. It is only possible to make an effort and inner consequences will always follow from effort." taken from *A Calendar of Wisdom*.

PART ONE

Chapter 1
The rain is pattering on the roof

'Tis my faith that every flower enjoys the air it breathes!
William Wordsworth

The heavy, meandering, spherical raindrops pounded a wild drumbeat on the tin roof of the old caravan. The windows were steamed up by the breath of the three men facing me. The first one stared at me over the rim of his thick, chipped white mug. The wisps of steam rose up giving him, in his opaque glasses, the look of a benign Mr Magoo.

His companion chewed his lip as he tapped out a soulless rhythm with his pencil on the old desk top. A brown suit, kipper tie and horn rimmed glasses marked him out as the boss. The third man was elderly and bald with mahogany skin from years spent out in all weathers. The corner of one side his mouth had the temerity to turn up when he thought nobody was looking.

"Could you repeat again, exactly, your request?" he insisted

"I rang two days ago and spoke to Geraldine" I started to explain.

A very nervous, young man in a brown overall had been dispatched to find the aforementioned Geraldine about five minutes before, but neither had returned.

I smothered a tickly cough in the thickening atmosphere and started again "I spoke to Geraldine a few days…" With that Geraldine rushed up the caravan steps breathless and with bosom heaving. I smiled at her and was fascinated by her blonde beehive held in place by an ornate, shiny Alice band. She had a definite look of Cindy Wilson, a member of the 1970s group the B52s.

The song "*Love Shack*" beat a distant drum in my head.

She glanced up at me over her red framed glasses and then said in beautifully modulated tones "I am so sorry you ended up in here, I was late into work this morning"

She rounded on the three protagonists. "This lady needs trees and plants, lots of them; she has an empty acre to fill and I said we could help her….Chop, chop."

I brought home a lot of the plants that day including forsythia, daphne, lilac, honeysuckle and the scented Mexican orange blossom as I wanted to make a start on planting as soon as I could.

The next day I headed for a fruit farm where they had agreed to see me. When I arrived they already had some trees tied up with rough green twine. The fruit farmer motioned me across and said "Apples, pears, plums and quinces, see what you can do with that lot"

I had explained to him on the phone the day before that I was setting up a garden from scratch. I unfolded the squashed forty pounds that we had agreed from my pocket. He put his hand up and said "Let this be my gift to you. Just make sure you plant them properly, my love" then he walked off. I struggled to get them into the back of the estate car but eventually managed it

The burlap sacks that the roots were encased in were sodden and my jeans and boots were ringing wet as I got back in my husband's estate car. "Whoops!" crossed my mind as I looked at the mess.

Chapter 2
How did I end up here?

Forgiveness is the fragrance that the violet sheds on the heel of that which has crushed it.

Mark Twain

My life had taken a complete about turn over the last few months. I was in my mid-thirties and had just moved my family from one end of the country to the other.

I had been married to a handsome, mercurial man, who I had known at school, since I was a teenager. He was in that exquisite path of a career trajectory that meant we followed him no matter what the consequences.

I had left my career, my extended family, my friends and my beautiful home to start a new life. More importantly I had uprooted my three children in their early teens and flung them unknowing into a distant place that might have well have been Mars.

In my defence what can I say? There was a particular kind of excitement in the air at that time in the middle of the 1980s and anything was possible. There seemed to be absolute certainties in life and I believed them all in my naivety. I believed that my husband had a career trajectory that could only continue to go up and that we would always be able to afford a nice house. I also believed that because I thought my husband was wonderful everyone else would appreciate his qualities.

I knew without doubt that the diagnoses of Multiple Sclerosis that I had received in my early twenties could be overcome if I concentrated hard enough and that I could stay forever at nine stone two pounds even if I kept eating chocolate in industrial quantities!

I had left my little blue mini with my brother in the Lakes as he had a young family to ferry around and I intended to buy a new car once we moved house.

However I was beginning to be really interested in green and environmental issues and so I had decided to walk everywhere, just very slowly.

I had always lived in rainy places such as Manchester, North Wales and The Lake District. I had also enjoyed holidays in rainy places such as Vancouver and Ireland but I had never encountered weather like they had in East Anglia.

The song *"Four Seasons in One Day"* by one of my favourite groups, Crowded House eloquently describes the climate there

You can wake up and when staring out of the window notice foggy, freezing gloom lying over the garden. As you run quickly to put the central heating on you remind your family to take a sweater with them when they go out. Then by lunchtime the sunshine is so strong you may need liberally applied factor thirty before you venture into the garden.

One morning we heard a noise that sounded like dozens of demented golfers throwing their hard, white missiles at our house. When we ran to the front door it was to see hailstones as big as golf balls landing on the cars that were parked on the large gravel drive.

The storm only lasted about two minutes but the work that was necessary to repair the dented roofs and bonnets on those cars took several weeks.

The flat, wheat coloured countryside in East Anglia means you could see for miles across the huge arable farms that surrounded our house. The perfect yellow of the rape seed crop meant that even those in our family who did not suffer from hay fever sneezed much more than they normally did.

Occasionally you would come across a field of bright red poppies that had taken over the wheat crop completely and the sight of the blood red carpet was shocking in its vibrancy. There was also a fad for growing flax on a small commune near our house and the bright blue of flowering flax once seen, was never to be forgotten.

Not long before we left the Lakeland Hills for our new home I interviewed a retired headmistress from Bungay in Suffolk about her pension entitlement.

I remarked that although I was looking forward to living in East Anglia, I found the flat open countryside a little disconcerting and would miss the green hills and valleys.

"Gosh" she said "I am moving up here to live with my son in Windermere but I find all these hills give me claustrophobia."

As my dear mother always remarked "It would not do if we were all the same."

One Sunday morning we were heading for the coast to let Bella our golden retriever do her favourite thing of running wildly in the freezing winter waves.

As we drove along a quiet road I said to Grant quietly,

"I wonder what these green crops are that would survive such cold winter"

"They look like brassicas of some...what the hell is that?" he replied as he stopped the car.

In front of us and to the left approaching fast was a real live whirlwind. We were as still as statues as we stared at the fast moving phenomenon. It was wide at the top and narrower at the bottom, and crossed our path as it disappeared noiselessly into the distance. There was not another soul around as the silence it left in its wake and slowly enveloped us.

As Grant started the car he said, "Thank goodness we do not live in Kansas."

We carried onwards to the empty wind swept beach that was our destination and threw dozens of stones for a deliriously happy, very sodden dog.

East Anglia is a beautiful place but the wind blowing from the North is ferocious and the downside of being in the fresh air all the time meant the joys of developing the dreaded acne rosacea on my face. That plus the crazy hairstyle I had developed by washing my hair in hard water made me wince when I looked in the mirror, so I had stopped looking at myself.

I loved gardening and felt that kneeling down and working the soil was very life affirming. I was not eating very much at that time and was getting thinner and thinner.

I really had stopped taking notice of the weather and was outside rain and shine, once the children had gone to school. One day the storm was never ending and when I came in for a late lunch I realised I my clothes were completely saturated.

I went in the house and then had a reviving shower before I went to collect my youngest son James from school. He had explained to me, after a geography lesson, that the water in East Anglia was described as hard which meant it percolated through deposits of limestone, chalk and calcium. The only thing I knew about it was it meant we needed more shampoo and washing powder and to replace the kettle more frequently. The worst thing though was that my perfect auburn bob looked just a little bedraggled no matter what I did with it!

Later on that evening we saw a piece on the ten o'clock news about the terrible nuclear disaster in Chernobyl. The nuclear reactor in that city in Northern Kiev had exploded causing the most single terrible incident in history of nuclear power. The staff who worked at the reactor lived in a village close by called Pripyat. Most workers were fast asleep when the incident happened and by the time they were evacuated hours later the majority had been affected by radiation poisoning.

There was talk on the radio of the rain bringing toxicity across to Europe and then the chance that it might make its way to the sheep farms in the high mountains.

About a week later to my deep consternation my precious hair started to fall out in handfuls. My husband asked me if I thought that I had been affected by the Chernobyl rainfall but I laughed and said I was convinced it was more to do with not eating very much and missing my mother!

CHAPTER 3
I think we are beginning to settle here

A daughter may outgrow your lap, but she will never outgrow your heart.

Anonymous

I think we stopped watching television as a family about the time we left the Lake District. The last thing I really remember us doing as a family was watching Bob Geldof's *Live Aid* the previous summer. Stars such as Phil Collins, Paul McCartney, U2, Mick Jagger, and David Bowie all joined in the spectacular live concerts from Wembley. That was when we realised that it got dark earlier in the South of England as we watched the flood lit concert from the bright evening sunshine our Lakeland home.

Television programmes such as *Lovejoy* which was set in East Anglia and the popular Liverpool family show *Bread* did not interest my teenage children or me for that matter. Radio Four was still a staple in our house.

Miranda, my daughter settled down immediately and loved her new life. She made two perfect friends on her first day, Megan and Helen and they have remained her best friends to this day. We lived amongst picturesque woodland of pine and silver birch and there were wide paths everywhere: for the first time she had the freedom to cycle to school and her friend's houses.

Fourteen year old girls seemed much younger in this part of the country but on the whole I decided that was no bad thing. There were school discos and local dances and Grant, my husband insisted on meeting our daughter outside every function she attended.

His perfect ruse for getting her out of anywhere on time was to go in and join the group she was dancing with until she nearly collapsed from embarrassment and ran outside.

He was brilliant as every weekend he was to be found waiting outside which ever place his children were hanging out, ready to take home as many kids as he could fit in his large estate car.

One evening Miranda arrived home looking a little chastened. Months before her Dad had removed his heavy wedding band as his many corporate lunches had made the fitting a little snug.

He had left the ring on the shelf in the bathroom and with his permission she had started wearing it on her thumb when she went out. One particular evening whilst executing a particularly difficult dance move which included flinging her arms in the air whilst twirling around the heavy platinum band had flown across the dance floor.

Despite the immediate appearance of the ever vigilant, village hall caretaker who turned all the lights on immediately the ring was never seen again.

Her doting father just smiled and said "It was just one of those things."

I actually did not deign buy him a new one until we were in a lovely jewellers shop in Las Vegas twenty years later.

I had designed for Miranda a beautiful lilac bedroom with a canopy bed and pale oak bedroom furniture. We were sitting chatting in there one warm evening, and I had on shorts and tee-shirt. I was just thinking what a perfect day it was when she screamed "Oh my goodness!"

"Whatever is the matter?" I enquired looking around us extremely alarmed.

"Oh Mum, your knees look just like chubby little babies bottoms" she squealed.

We both fell about laughing and I thought to myself,

"Nobody in the world can sock it to you like a teenage daughter!"

James, my youngest son had become very quiet and I knew he was finding his new school very impersonal. I went to see his head teacher but he seemed very disinterested and cold and the PTA seemed non-existent. I lay awake at night worrying that we had done the wrong thing by uprooting the children.

There was a very strange incident at the Parents Evening when it became obvious that his young teacher was having a serious breakdown in front of a room full of parents. I knew that he was South African and had taught in Soweto and that was where he seemed to think he was on that snowy night in rural East Anglia.

Grant, who had been a school governor for years, got up quietly and went to speak to the Head Teacher. The Parents evening was abandoned and fortunately the young man got the help he needed and went back home to spend some time with his family.

I had been very involved in all the children's schools before we moved house and wanted to be included again. In the quiet of the long nights I just hoped and prayed that we were providing them with a better future even though at that moment I felt we were on shaky ground.

When we first moved into our new house our oldest son Theo was five foot four inches tall. Three months later he was six foot three inches in height.

I soon came to realise that the move was the worst thing we could have done to him.

He changed completely in that first year. Teenage boys do change of course but I knew this was more than that. His right shoulder was raised in a permanent shrug of insouciance and if you looked hard you could see the snarl of indifference that played about his mouth.

However it was his eyes that told the story. His familial green eyes with dark lashes had always been full of laughter: now they were cool as iced water.

A teenager turns from a boy to a man in a heartbeat. His voice drops into manhood and he wants to be free, but of what he has no idea: but certainly from a mother that wants him to obey the rules. Theo was really engaging sometimes and helped me dig a fish pond in the garden and paint the kitchen.

He was well behaved at school even though I knew he felt like a visitor from another planet with his height, his Northern accent and his powerful intellect.

I was a slender thirty-five year old with two younger children and an unrealistic picture book view of family life. I was determined to keep to the routine that had served us so well before the move. I wanted everybody to keep obeying the rules by handing their homework in on time and Theo and I bumped heads a lot.

I loved him so much but the days of holding him close to me were over forever.

My husband should have been a powerful ally at this point but along with most men in their thirties with a high flying job, his mind was elsewhere even if his body was present.

He was good at running football teams and helping with the scouts but talking about the stuff that boys need to talk about was not part of his skill set.

Most mothers believe that if they try hard enough things will improve and on the whole they usually do. However unless you can look at the bigger picture then you may be trying too hard in completely the wrong direction.

I was absolutely determined we would be a perfect family and the things that were going wrong were just a temporary aberration. I was using my heart to deal with the problems as they arrived when I should have been using my head.

CHAPTET 4
Life in another place

The great advantage of living in a large family is that early lesson in life's essential unfairness.

Nancy Mitford

Life settled into a rhythm and one pleasant day began to follow another. The children had their routines and life had a peaceful rhythm. Well it would have done if it were not for the exhausting disagreements between my two oldest children. It was always about something or it was about nothing, it really did not matter.

Interestingly in all the years I have worked as a therapist I often ask women the question "Do you get on with your brother?"

Depending on whether the answer is yes or no I can more or less tell you whether the brother is younger or older.

In most cases girls adore their younger brothers but would fight with older brothers until the last breathe. I have come to the conclusion it is just the way nature intends it to be!

The house was always full of young people and we always had at least a dozen for Sunday lunch. One evening Miranda came into the kitchen and perched on the kitchen counter. I recognised that all the children had signals when they wanted to talk and this was hers. We went round the houses a few times and eventually I said to her "Whatever is the matter, love?"

She told me in a quiet voice that one of the girls in her class was pregnant and had not told her mother. I asked her who it was and she mentioned the name of the sweetest, brainiest girl in the class. I asked how far along she was and then said "I really need to see her".

A week later she still had not been round to our house and so I said to my daughter "We are going away for a few days next week and I want to see Pippa before we go".

The next evening when I came in from work I pushed the kitchen door open and there she was, pale and anxious. I held her tight and then said "There is no way round this sweetie, your mum has to know about the baby." She looked at me from behind her serious round glasses.

"Please, please will you come with me to see her?" she asked.

We arranged that she would come to our house in the morning and I would drive her back home to talk to her mother. The next morning Grant took the children to school and I sat at the kitchen table talking quietly to Pippa about what she wanted to do with her life.

As we drove away from our house Madonna's "Poppa don't Preach" was on the radio and we turned to each other and smiled a wry smile.

I held her hand tightly but I was very nervous too as I pulled up on the drive and left the pale young woman in the car.

I did not know her mother well enough to know how she would react. To her credit she was calm and poised as I conveyed the news. We went out to get her beautiful daughter out of the car and I left the two of them with their heads together in the doorway. My heart ached for them both.

As I drove on towards my office I thought about how I would have reacted if it had been my daughter. I like to think I would have been calm but if I was honest I suspected I would have been much more agitated and would have felt very guilty that I had missed the signs.

That lovely young woman became a perfect mother. She graduated whilst bringing up a wonderful daughter. Her energy and determination astounded me and they both still have a really special place in my heart.

James made friends with the local newspaper editor's son. They were nice people and made James welcome in their home as we did with their son who was called Mark. Grant started up a football team and his company sponsored the league.

A retired international footballer who had a son about the same age as James came to help coach the team and slowly they improved and climbed up the league. My husband would be the first to admit he had very little in the way footballing skills but always insisted in giving all the boys a turn even if they were not very good!

This did not always please the phalanx of pushy parents who manned the touch line. Their insistence that the better players deserved the places did not cut any ice with Grant. He continued to give all the boys a turn and returned the unhelpful remarks with his haughty glare.

Our oldest son Theo had always had it in his plans that he wanted to work in the City. The careers officer had advised him to think about marine biology because that was his favourite subject. However the news of the Big Bang in the City caught his attention and he explained to me that deregulation meant the markets were opened up for the first time.

There was a series on television about the City called *Capital City* with Douglas Hodge and he loved watching it. I wondered whether he would be deflected from his plan but doubted it knowing how determined his character was.

I had worried so much about how my family would settle but now there were days now where I felt relaxed from morning until night.

CHAPTER 5
"Mum, I just saw Father Christmas

I will honour Christmas in my heart and try to keep it all year.
Charles Dickens

With our first Christmas in East Anglia approaching we decided to go up to the Lakes on Christmas Day and we did not see another soul on the road except for a fully decked out Father Christmas with his head under the bonnet on the M6.

The week before the holidays began Grant and I had gone to a famous fish restaurant on the Suffolk coast for a wonderful meal. We had both had different menus and when he offered me one of his oysters I ate it without thinking. I had never had one before as quite frankly I thought they looked disgusting!

It was the most fun I had had since we moved and I felt really close to him. The next day I was just about to make lunch when I felt a horrible pain in my stomach. I just about managed to get up to my bedroom when with a bump I landed on the floor. The children were all home from school and so I did not need to be anywhere. It was a good job because it was forty eight hours before I got up again.

I was so ill that day with what turned out to be an allergy to oysters. Miranda rang Grant and he came home. He looked at me and then his watch and said "Do you want me to get a doctor?"

I muttered the eternal female answer into the cream bedroom carpet "I am alright, thank you". He tutted, tapped his foot on the floor and went off to do his important work. I actually know he tapped his foot as it was the part of him that was nearest my pasty green face.

Two days later, shaken and pale I resumed Christmas preparations. The relief on his face when Grant came home to find me up and about was obvious. I felt very hurt that he had not taken enough care of me and when I thought about it I realised that it was going to be that way in the future.

We had fun that Christmas but as the children spent time with their friends they began to realise that life moves on. I enjoyed being with my whole family but especially with my small nieces and nephews and we laughed a lot that year.

The day after Boxing Day I went shopping for my mother and I borrowed my brother's little blue mini that was parked on her drive. I ran round the supermarket and got back in the car and then drove back home.

As the familiar car stopped I bent down to turn off the radio and then looked up. To my absolute horror I was sitting on the drive of my perfect house that I had sold only three months before. It was the house that I had lived in very happily for the last eight years. My unconscious mind had taken me on a journey that I had been on thousands of times before.

My face was red and hot with embarrassment and I looked around wildly. It was very fortunate that the new owners were not home that day and as I put the car into reverse I really noticed my beautiful home.

Whilst I was living there I had planted perfect blue conifers interspersed with yellow standard roses all around the front lawn. I had also fitted expensive up to the minute vertical cream blinds at all the windows.

As I looked back I realised that the beautiful plants and lawns were gone and had been replaced with cold grey concrete and the blinds had been replaced by ubiquitous dull net curtains.

I learned a valuable lesson that day, just because you think something is wonderful does not mean everyone else is going to agree with you!

As the New Year began I had a relapse of my illness and spent most of the day resting when the family was out. I hoped it would pass as that is what happens with the relapsing and remitting MS. You just have to sit it out and hope for better days. It took me all my time to run the house and see to the family but taking things slowly seemed to be the fastest way of repairing my broken body. Thank goodness as Easter approached I was beginning to feel good again and life moved on.

With lots of help I spent my free time turning a featureless muddy patch into a lovely verdant acre garden with a prolific vegetable patch that fed the whole family.

My oldest son, Theo still hated vegetables and I did what I had always done since he was four years old. I tipped his portion of carrots, cabbage, broccoli or kale into the blender added some gravy on top and then poured the whole thing over his dinner.

Every time we sat down he always asked "Is there wine in this gravy, Mum?" I would answer truthfully "Of course not dear" and he would eat the lot.

Vitamin intake intact and heated argument nicely avoided.

CHAPTER 6
My Grandmother Alexandra

When grandmothers enter the door, discipline flies out of the window.
Ogden Nash

My father Murray rang to tell me that his mother Alexandra had died. Although we both felt sad, we agreed that she had lived a long and full life. She had been eighty-six and drifting away peacefully in your sleep seemed a good way to go as any. He gave me the date and time of the funeral and wishing him well we said our goodbyes.

I felt a little shaken and after making myself a cup of earl grey tea I settled down in the garden under the newly planted arbour with the imaginary roses to remember her life and what she had meant to me.

Grandmother Alexandra had been born in 1904; the youngest of five children all born close together. A boy George had been quickly followed by four sisters Gladys, Evelyn, Florence and Alexandra. Their older Victorian father Arthur, complete with handlebar moustache, owned a factory in Manchester and their delicate, pretty mother Phyllis was a homemaker. They lived in a lovely Georgian house with a large garden opposite a park in central Manchester. It was a perfect, pleasure filled childhood.

When Alexandra was ten years old all this came crashing to an unhappy end. At about the time of the start of the First World War in 1914 her adored father died suddenly of heart failure. Not long afterwards seventeen year old George had to leave the family home to join the army to fight for his country.

The four girls were left alone with their distraught mother. The two oldest girls Gladys and Evelyn had just started work and Florence and Alexandra were still at school.

Their mother Phyllis tried to run the factory but all was not as it had seemed financially and eventually it had to be sold at a meagre profit. The knock on the door that signalled the loss of George in the trenches was too much to bear and she died two months later of a broken heart.

The oldest daughter Gladys was already engaged to a young man from New Zealand and she soon left the country leaving the three sisters to cope alone. She lived in New Zealand for the rest of her life and never had any children.

Their late father's financial trouble was worse than first thought and their lovely house had to be sold. The three sisters moved into a rented house in another part of town and Florence and Evelyn worked whilst Phyllis finished school. They were alone in the world and had gone from a life of ease to one of penury in a very short time.

Life moved on and eventually Evelyn married and had one son. She was the least kind of all the sisters and lived into her nineties. I remember an elderly lady in a green velvet hat worn at a rakish angle and bright orange lipstick that had been applied without the aid of a pair of glasses or a mirror!

I really tried to like her because of my belief in the innate goodness of all people. However my Father's stories of being forced as a small boy to sit at the table for hours until he finished his terrible boiled cabbage made this difficult.

Florence was the only sister left at home with Alexandra and they were content and cheerful. Florence was the kindest sister by far and looked after her younger sister well. When Alexandra was eighteen and Florence twenty three they both fell in love at the same time. Florence married first and went on to have a dozen children.

They were all very sporty and two of her sons played for Manchester City Football club.

Alexandra married William, handsome, charming and a little unreliable. A year later she gave birth to my father, Murray. They lived happily but just after their daughter Eileen was born seven years later, William began to have an affair with her best friend.

The young woman Rose had come to stay with them when her husband had left her and within months she and William had disappeared into the night, never to be seen again.

His whereabouts were unknown although once he was an adult my father searched for his father for many years. It was not until the year 2000 when he was seventy five that Murray discovered that his father had actually lived only a mile away from him when he was a child. This was completely possible in the days when nobody travelled very far from home and people treated minding their own business as an art form.

Whilst doing a project for a University course my Aunt Eileen's daughter Polly discovered that Grandfather William had died of a brain tumour at the age of forty.

His new family of a son and a daughter had moved with their mother to make a life in New Zealand. There was some contact and an invitation to visit them but I do not think it ever materialised.

CHAPTER 7
What Grandmother Alexandra did next?

Grandmothers are mums with a lot of frosting.
Anonymous

Alexandra was left high and dry with two small children and the fact was that she had absolutely no income. She took a job as a housekeeper for a ruddy faced, moustachioed middle aged man called Mr Peacock. He appeared not to have a first name. His wife had died and he had a daughter the same age as my Aunt Eileen and he was happy to take the girl into his house but not the boy.

At the age of seven my father was taken into care and sent to a boy's school in Southport. He always said "It gave me a good education and a determined spirit" but I know he never got over the abandonment. Mr Peacock and Alexandra eventually fell in love and married.

At fourteen Murray left the children's home and was welcomed with open arms at Mr Peacock's house, as of course he could now earn a wage. He lived there with his mother and sister until he joined the Royal Marines at seventeen. He had been introduced to my mother Mona when he was sixteen and he said that this was the day his life began.

Mr Peacock died about the time my aunt got married and so Alexandra was on her own again. She loved travel and excitement and on the way back from a solo trip to the seaside she met her third husband and the man I knew as Grandfather, Hubert M.Smyth.

When Mother and Father married they went to live with her and when Hubert asked Alexandra to marry him she left them there and moved into Hubert's house in north Manchester.

My Grandmother Alexandra loved life, she smiled and laughed and treated each day as if it were brand new. Nothing ever bothered her and she was always ready for adventure. She did the minimum of housework and cooking. Her salads had to be checked diligently and surreptitiously for caterpillars and the water from the cooked vegetables was cooled and then drunk by her as though it was the finest champagne.

When she was fifty seven years old Hubert died suddenly. Their home was a tied cottage that belonged to Hubert's previous employer. She was expected to move out within the week. Father and I went to his funeral and brought Alexandra back with us to stay for a little while. Of course there was very little room in our tiny home but she needed a bed and so I slept on the sofa for a while until Father was able to find her an apartment close by.

She made friends on her first day in her new home and with them she continued to travel. She was kind and cheerful and I never heard offer a contrary opinion about anything to anybody. Her curly silver hair framed her pretty unlined face and her pink cheeks meant people just adored her.

However when I once asked her why she had abandoned my father at seven years old she just stared at me for a while then shrugged with insouciance and began to talk about the weather. I had always loved her dearly but something in my heart definitely shifted that day.

At eighty years old she moved into a wonderful retirement home in the Lakeland countryside that was owned by some family friends. She continued to enjoy her life being looked after and fussed over by anyone and everyone. She died at eighty six years old without a line on her face and with a gentle smile on her lips.

CHAPTER 8
Happy Heidelberg adventure

Each day provides its own gifts.
Marcus Aurelius

In the spring of the following year we were invited to go on a business conference trip to Heidelberg in Germany. I was thankful that the date of the trip was a month before Theo's seventeenth birthday as I knew once he passed his driving test I would not be able to tie him down.

I felt that the children were too young to leave alone and so with bated breath, I rang my mother to ask if she would come and stay. To my delight she answered in the affirmative and I told Grant I could go with him on his business trip.

I was so excited and I enjoyed getting my clothes ready for the formal week ahead. The day arrived and my parents pulled up in the drive. We were delighted to see them as we missed living in the same neighbourhood and we exchanged family news.

The next morning we set off for Gatwick to meet the marvellous crowd we usually travelled with on these trips. We had been to Rome with them the year before and had a great time eating, drinking and laughing until dawn. Globe artichokes dripping in butter, Fettuccine Alfredo, Saltimbocca and Spaghetti Carbora were some of my favourite dishes.

There were two things I cherished from the Italian trip. One was the marvellous sight from the hotel balcony, of scores of Catholic priests dressed in black boarding coaches to take them to the Vatican. Then their spectacular return, dressed in Bishop's deepest purple, as the settling dusk was busy painting the sky a similar hue.

The next day a smaller groups of purple clad Bishops left to return hours later in the most startling scarlet of the Cardinal's robes. This was a heart stopping sight for our group who were on the terrace taking in the evening air.

We were told that Cardinal red represented the blood of Christ, the Bishop's purple royalty and the priests black poverty.

The other thing I treasured was the advice of the moustached elderly guide who took us around the city of Rome. Flourishing his furled navy umbrella aloft he advised "Always make eye contact with the man whose car you are about to cross in front of, as he is less likely to run you over that way!"

At the airport I could see elegant Joanna with her cheerful husband Brian from Blackpool. Then I spied Jack, tall and bespectacled and his attractive television presenter wife Julie.

The Managing Director of the French arm of the Oil Company my husband worked for was travelling with us and he had always adored Julie.

He had been heard to remark in heavily accented English, "She has a personality that can light up the back of a coach."

I am afraid wondering what that might look like gave me a fit of the giggles and I had to go and stand in the ladies until I composed myself. I adored our wonderful good friends John and Jackie and was looking forward to catching up. They were both larger than life and always invited us to their box at Ascot each year.

The flight was uneventful and our hotel in Germany was five stars but there was not a minute to relax as we were rushed out to a beer kellar and the promised local entertainment. Grant was the first speaker at the conference the next day so I advised him to go carefully with the Steins of beer.

They would have been fine on their own but we were fed sausage and fermenting cabbage in the form of sauerkraut to the accompanying sounds of loud oom-pah-pah music. Grant spent all night rolling about the bed and moaning about how he was never coming back to Germany, before he pulled himself together for the next day.

The trouble was that although it was spring the snow was falling hard and the wind was howling all around. The ladies in their finery were treated to a trip into the mountains where we were shown a beautiful view. Well it would have been beautiful if the fog was not so dense, as we stood on the balcony and stared at a white outside, shivering.

The afternoon we met up with the chaps and went on a coach trip to a wine tasting event at a vineyard. They may have been making Eiswein or ice wine for all I knew because we were all absolutely frozen. A lot of people stayed inside and I think copious quantities of wine were consumed that afternoon.

We were late back on the coach to be in time for our evening's entertainment at Heidelberg Castle so everyone was advised to rush. Some poor elderly chap rushed so hard and combined with all the wine he had consumed slipped heavily in the shower and was taken to hospital with suspected concussion.

We were now all in our eveningwear as we piled back into the coach. Our frazzled party of fifty, chilly, overdressed people climbed out of our warm vehicle and waited at the bottom of the castle steps waiting to be drummed in by the regal, brass band. Well we waited and waited and nothing happened.

Some of the men were taking their evening jackets off to keep the ladies warm. The occasional wag was heard to say that it might have been better to be warm in hospital with suspected concussion than stood on these freezing stone steps.

Eventually the colourful horsemen and trumpeting drummers arrived and we were escorted up the steps into the dining hall. Long benches and seats awaited us like some medieval form of torture. We all sat down and moaned a lot and could not actually see who was opposite because of the stygian gloom that surrounded us.

Pretty young fräuleins dressed as serving wenches, gave us brown earthenware bowls with something hot and wet inside. We knew it was wet because it dribbled out of the cracks and on to our evening finery. We knew it was hot because of some of the guests who could be heard shouting "Ouch, ouch damn!" into the gloom.

We were promised an authentic experience so the next thing that arrived was a piece of roasted meat. It was plonked from the serving dish straight onto the wooden table with a resounding slap and neither a knife or a fork arrived with which to eat the delightful dish. The meat juices dribbled slowly and unceremoniously on to the floor as the seated guests swivelled their well-dressed knees from side to side to protect their evening wear.

The assemble guests were all whispering that things could not get any worse when the plumed horses began their show. A huge white horse in all its finery backed up in the dark towards our table. I could see the funny side of this, but Irene, whose husband had organised the event, had really had enough of the whole thing.

Just as she raised herself to her full five feet height to wave and try to attract her husband's attention the white horse jiggled further backwards and released the most explosive case of trapped wind that I had ever heard.

Irene collapsed on the floor like a heroine in a Jane Austin novel and I think the German equivalent of smelling salts was administered. I definitely heard "Gib die Dame 'ne Adrenalinspritze" and so I think that was what it was on offer.

Her devoted husband came rushing over to rescue her and our whole party were marched on to the coach and were going back to the hotel ten minutes later.

We got back to the hotel and medicinal brandies were ordered for the assembled company. The bungled German castle experience was never to be spoken of again in the annals of that particular oil company.

CHAPTER 9
Can you see that Schloss?

The privilege of a lifetime is being who you are.
Joseph Campbell

The following day we were summoned for a boat ride down the Rhine and it was totally mesmeric as we sailed along in luxury. The Necker River valley with its ancient castles or schlosses clinging to the hillside proved to be some of the most beautiful I had ever seen. The grapevines looked sparkling and frothily green in the sunlight. We passed Germany's oldest University at Heidelberg

It was founded in 1836 and the sandstone ruins of beautiful Heidelberg Castle were magnificent. The red rooftops of the town are best viewed from the river and the day was bright and warm as we sailed along. We were served white wine and nibbles as the delicious day floated slowly by.

When we got back to the hotel in the evening there was another coach waiting to take us to a banquet. We were told that we needed to be ready in forty minutes. We got back to the hotel room and I flopped on the bed and asked Grant to fix me a drink. I remember it fizzed and the faint scent of juniper berries tickled my nose and then, well nothing at all....

The next thing I knew was that I was staring into Grant's wild eyes. "Hurry up, love, you have been asleep, the coach goes in five minutes. I was downstairs talking to the crowd and thought you were getting ready"

"Oh crikey!" I thought "here we go again".

I ran through the steaming shower drops holding my hair up with my left hand. I forced my damp body into screamingly, resistant underwear and dragged a vaguely suitable long red dress off a hanger.

As I ran out of the door towards the lift I pulled my emergency makeup bag out of my handbag. The thirty second lift ride saw me apply my plum Ester Lauder lipstick and run my fingers through my hair. I stepped out of that lift with my best conference smile firmly stuck on my face.

The restaurant was spacious and elegant and as I first made small talk first to my left and then to my right. I really hoped the main course was going to be delicious. I had been to so many occasions where men in tuxedos and women in splendid evening dresses were offered the kind of food that should only be eaten behind closed doors.

The creamy vegetable soup arrived with a puff pastry lid and as diners tenuously lifted it to expose the liquid contents, those with glasses looked like Mr Magoo and those without glasses just got very smarty eyes. Any woman daring to rub her eyes then gave a good approximation of a startled panda with smudged mascara, as the waterproof kind had not been invented then.

Finally the star of the show arrived with all the pomp and ceremony befitting its status in German society. When the waiters lifted the silver domes there sat huge plates of white asparagus dripping with creamy butter.

I looked round and you could see my fellow diner's confusion as to how they were going to eat this. "Blow this, I do not care anymore" I thought as I decided to tuck in without a care for the consequences. Butter dripped down all our chins as we enjoyed the delicious fare and we laughed all the way back to the hotel. Our final morning included a leisurely breakfast or Frühstuck consisting of typical deli fare including dark breads, eggs, ham and delicious sausages of every variety.We lingered so long over our coffee that there was a mad rush for the airport so that we were in time for our plane.

When we arrived back home from the German business trip the family had been having a wonderful time and my father had kindly done lots of work for me in my precious garden.

My parents stayed with us for Easter. I loved the Easter holidays and put as much effort into making them special as I did Christmas.

To decorate the house with fresh greenery and spring flowers was such fun. Parrot Tulips, Hyacinths and Lily of the Valley poured their exquisite scent all over the house. I spent a lovely hour in the kitchen making coloured eggs by boiling them in onion skins whilst I listened to the radio. I looked out of my kitchen window to see all the family sitting under the rose and wisteria covered arbour in the spring sunshine. It felt wonderful to have my parents there with my children.

I spent a day baking and made a traditional Simnel cake with almond paste and then crafted handmade Easter Eggs which were a little wonky but all the better for it.

I thought about all the years when the children were small and we always had a brisk walk round Tarn Hows near Coniston on Good Friday. We always took a flask of hot chocolate and homemade hot cross buns with us for sustenance. We alternated decorating the tops of hot cross buns between drawing a cross with a butter knife and rolling out pastry for the top. I discovered early on that small children like to roll out pastry, bigger ones like the economy of effort that a butter knife produces.

It gave me a whisper of disappointment to think that these days were now behind us as a family.

Easter Sunday dinner was always a large free range turkey as there was a poultry farm in the next village. The vegetables came from the garden and to finish after the local cheeses was always a famous raspberry trifle. The recipe for this delicious concoction consisting of layers of fruit, jelly, custard and fresh cream sprinkled with flaked almonds had been passed down through the family from Great Grandmother Hannah.

I had always grown my own vegetables and I always froze the produce we did not eat at once. By this time of year I had to go searching with a torch and the step ladder to find the elusive last green striped bag of plump raspberries hidden under a box of string beans.

I was really grateful to my parents for whatever the teenage equivalent of babysitting was called and felt so sad when they set off on the long journey home to the Lakes.

My heart actually ached as their drove out along the drive and away into the flat, wheat coloured countryside. I stood for a long time after their car had disappeared from my view lost in my own thoughts.

CHAPTER 10
I am going back to work

Common sense is that which judges the things given to it by other senses.
Leonardo da Vinci

I had a great year off work and really was beginning to feel well again. I enjoyed domesticity and the tasks involved in making my new home look perfect. The salty tears that I shed because I missed my old life had dried and I felt much more in control.

All the children had finally settled and had good social lives and seemed to be doing well at school. I very rarely saw Grant as he was so busy but I was often invited to glamorous occasions where he was guest of honour and I was the woman who smiled and chatted as she worked the room.

If I am honest I loved those experiences of being presented with a perfect bouquet and the feeling of looking elegant and important, even if it was diametrically opposite to my own working life that was spent dealing with other people's problems.

Through the years I had suffered through so many company dinners waiting for the guests of honour to arrive and now we were the important guests I liked to be sure we did not keep people waiting.

My health had improved dramatically and I was wondering when I should go back to work as, in truth, we really missed my salary. My mind was made up the day I went to the races at the famous Newmarket course.

It was a beautiful sunny day with the lightest of breezes and a crowd of vibrant and interesting companions. As usual I was driving and so I accompanied my delicious lunch of lamb and spring vegetables with mineral water.

A rather rotund, red-faced customer had decided to regale me with his life story. I love people and usually enjoyed hearing these stories but I had a very strong feminist streak and hated chauvinism in all its varieties.

There was some talk of the next race which we were watching from the dining room. My companion turned to me and said "Have you brought your child benefit book, love?"

My first instinct was to pour my green bottle of perfectly chilled Perrier water on his bald pate. I smiled wanly and excused myself as I moved away.

We had a lovely afternoon but Grant could tell by the set of my jaw that something was wrong on the way home.

"The time is right" I muttered "I am going to see the office manager tomorrow and start work as soon as I can"

I made an appointment and the next afternoon after a short interview was offered a job. The manager frowned as he read my references and said "The new round of Executive Officer exams is on in London next week, do you want me to put you forward?"

I thanked him and found myself sitting the exams a few days later. The building where the exams were held was in London. After a morning of using my rather rusty brain, I took a black cab into the West End and treated myself to a walk around Harrods. Whilst buying myself some perfume I thought "Yes, I am ready to face the world again".

As I was waiting for the return of my credit card I stared at my hands. I realised they were the hands of a gardener, red and sore with chipped cracked nails.

Horrified by what I saw I made a mental note to go to Boots to buy a jar of Smiths Creamola. This had been my trusted potion for great hands since I was a teenager.

The perfume I chose that day was Tresor by Lancôme as it was my Mother's favourite modern scent. I bought two of the unusual shaped glass bottles, one for her and one for myself. She also liked Chanel No 5 but that was to be kept for special occasions which were few and far between.

The next week I was delighted to hear I had passed the exam and when I started my new job it was in a management and training position that I absolutely loved.

I thought to myself, isn't life funny? "If I had not gone to the races that particular day, I would not have this perfect job."

I felt a bit guilty going back to work but the children were all in their teens and very capable. I hired a lovely local lady, Jean, to do the ironing and some of the housework. We were surrounded by woodland and Jean's husband Simon was the local gamekeeper.

I had never had anyone to help me in the house before as my mother was absolutely set against it. In Mother's opinion having someone else to do your housework was a sign of moral turpitude.

I don't really know what that said about my character but I absolutely adored having more free time and a tidy house!

The balance of my marriage began to improve dramatically as well. Grant had acquired that patina of self-importance that successful men have. Now I was back earning a living he seemed to regard my opinions as having more validity which was better all around.

There are many profound differences between men and women. In my opinion men seem to judge each other by the cars they own, whereas the first thing women seem to look at is each other's jewellery. Men define themselves by their careers and change their personality with each step up the ladder. If they unfortunately lose their job it can have a devastating effect on the rest of their lives.

Women tend to define themselves by their personal lives and are pretty much the same no matter how powerful they are in the workplace.

I tried to teach my children that there is no success without failure and if you fall down you just get up again and get on with it. If I ever started on a discussion that appeared to be heading that way, they would shout "We know, we know, Mum, there is more than one way up a mountain!"

One evening I got home from work to find Miranda and Grant in the kitchen and they stopped talking as I opened the door. I sighed and put my bag on the dresser next to the sherry decanter. "Good idea" I thought to myself and poured a drop of the amber liquid into a tiny crystal glass. I swallowed it in one gulp and felt the warmth radiate around my chest.

"OK, give it to me" I sighed. I turned round and they were both falling about with silent laughter.

"I have taken a decision" said Grant rather self-importantly "and decided that Miranda can have a scooter. We have been to the store and put a deposit down and we are going to collect it tomorrow".

I took a deep breath and put my hands behind me to steady myself on the dresser where I was still leaning. I closed my eyes and a faint scent of Seville oranges from the fruit bowl reached my nose.

I opened my eyes and smiled at Miranda and turned my attention to my husband. "I do not want to be difficult here but can I remind you what happened recently."

I knew that he knew what had happened to Miranda's friend Julia about a month before.

She had been waiting at a pedestrian crossing near the swimming baths when a large bus, whose driver had not seen her, knocked her and her scooter flying into the air. She had spent several days in hospital.

I smiled at Miranda again and shrugged my shoulders in a gesture of incomprehension.

"Alright, alright it was worth a try," she laughed, "why do you think I asked my Dad, I knew I would never get it passed the authorities" and then she skipped out of the room.

"Why, oh why, I am I always the person who has to be the bad guy in this house, could you take a turn once in a while, please" I said to his fast disappearing back. I never found out whether he got his deposit back.

I had developed three unbreakable rules for my teenagers.

1) Never, ever lie to me. If I know the truth I can always help you.

2) Never, ever tell me you are going one place and then go another as I want to be able to trust you.

3) Never, ever be late home without letting me know that there is a problem as my imagination will run riot!

All the other stuff from childhood counted as well of course. The normal rules about politeness, honesty, kindness and doing your homework still applied.

I found my three teenager's rules helped me, as a real worrier, negotiate the minefield that being a parent of teenagers appeared to have become.

CHAPTER 11
Dubrovnik is a lovely place

Those who seek paradise on earth should come to Dubrovnik.
George Bernard Shaw

We thought we needed a week's family holiday and it seemed to be that the consensus of opinion was that we should try Dubrovnik in Yugoslavia. Whilst waiting at the airport the sound of Terence Trent D'arby's *Wishing Well* was everywhere and the children rushed off to buy sweets and magazines for the journey. The two and a half hours went quickly by and we were soon landing at our holiday destination.

Dubrovnik, in the extreme south of Croatia, is known as the Pearl of the Adriatic and richly deserves its title. The hotel where we were staying was only two miles from Dubrovnik and our villa was set on the tree lined hillside with a path down to the beach. The first morning our walk for breakfast across the hotel grounds took us nearly an hour as we were all so captivated by the view across the ocean.

As we entered the hotel foyer Miranda picked up a pile of leaflets and as we waited for our coffee to arrive she began to read.

"Dubrovnik stands nestled between the Adriatic and Dinaric Alps and was a rich and powerful city state until the year 1806. The city has a population of over 100,000 and was once known as Ragusa.

George Bernard Shaw was enchanted by this beautiful city, about which he said "those who seek paradise on Earth should come to Dubrovnik", as well as, famously, describing it as "the pearl of the Adriatic". The Old Town became a Unesco World Heritage Site in 1979 and bore the scars of many battles. For centuries Yugoslavia was part of the Ottoman Empire then the Austro Hungarian Empire. The country received international recognition in July 1922 and was called South Slavic People"

She took a breath and for a moment we all thought she had finished.

"Dubrovnik has a borderline subtropical climate…"

"Stop, stop, stop" yelled her brothers in tandem "we cannot take anymore."

I looked across at my fifteen year old daughter dressed in the height of fashion but perhaps not so suitably for a relaxed holiday breakfast. Immaculate as always she had on a large blue shirt over leggings that were tucked into short grey boots. The bright blue of the shirt, which seemed to be short at the front and long at the back, set off her beautiful brown eyes and her long curly auburn hair tumbled artfully around her shoulders.

She gave her brothers a withering look. "The Bura wind blows uncomfortably cold and gusts down the Adriatic coast between October and April"…she looked at me with her teenage lips pursed into disapproval and said "You did not tell me it was windy here, what about my hair?"

Her brothers were collapsed in a fit of giggles at her discomfiture when our breakfast arrived.

We spent a week wandering around this lovely place. Grant had decided this was to be a week of public transport and discovery and so we took a boat trip to Korcula Island and wandered about the old town. We also took a bus trip to the Albanian border and marvelled at the countryside.

Then we walked into Dubrovnik itself to see the Aquarium and clamber on the historic city walls. The food was typically Mediterranean with fish dishes, stews and vegetables being plentiful.

The ice-cream, cakes and fresh fruit that finished every meal were certainly enjoyed by us all. Stands of huge watermelons were everywhere and were a perfect way to quench our thirsts if we had been walking. The children were all keen tennis players and after a losing battle with the Brura winds we had such fun playing every single day.

All too soon it was time to leave this magical place and who was to know that within a few shorts years the already scarred walls would bear further evidence of modern battles for this beautiful, haunting city.

CHAPTER 12
A lovely evening

No bird soars to high if he soars with his own wings.
William Blake

Later that same October, one morning I woke up very early as I had left the window ajar in the night and the early morning birdsong was winding its sonorous way into my sleepy brain. The sparkling symphony was not only calling the birds to sing but it had summoned me too.

Five am found me working away in the garden. I loved these early hours on the vegetable patch when I could choose what to have to accompany that nights supper.

I had checked in on the children and they were all fast asleep and that delicious sense of early morning peace was pervading the whole house. As the clock ticked, our golden retriever Bella and our elderly ginger cat Fudge were fast asleep by the Aga and did not stir as I waited for the coffee to brew.

I had been grocery shopping the evening before and the warm kitchen was full of good things. On the pine dresser sat a Majolica dish of fat, purple plums and when you peered closer you could discern the bloom on their skin and catch the intoxicating scent of autumn. A jute sack of red apples was propped in the corner that had been delivered by to us by Mr Timms, a friendly neighbour from down the lane.

As I gazed through the widow at my beautiful garden, my eyes rested for a moment on my mother's antique copper jug, full of purple chrysanthemums that I had picked the day before.

The air was like wine that morning as I knelt to lift the brightly coloured impatiens from their summer home. They had made a spectacular show all through the summer in their beds against the old brick wall that wound sedately around the front garden. The mellow ancient brickwork acted as a storage heater for the espaliers of peaches and figs that I had planted up against its whole length. I chose the best dozen specimens of impatiens and planted them neatly in pots ready to take into the office.

Government offices are always very grey and utilitarian and so I loved to take in plants to brighten the work environment. I did not take in flowers as I had learned my lesson early on.

A colleague had gone on holiday leaving a vase of dahlias on her office window ledge. To comply with a recent time management survey I had been tasked with filling in a report of my whereabouts every half hour. This was going to be tricky as my job involved a lot of running around between two grey, utilitarian twelve story buildings. I was immaculately dressed that particular day in a black dress and high heels as we were expecting a visit from the Minister of State.

I had made sure the office was in order the night before but I when I arrived early the next morning the office was empty. I went round and opened the blinds until I could no longer ignore what my nose was telling me.

There was a terrible smell somewhere in the office and I had no idea where it was coming from.

I sniffed here and there and as people arrived I had them joining me in a crazy game of "Please get rid of the smell before the dignitary arrives".

One hour later, there was a loud shout of "Ha, Ha!" from a rather severe lady called Elizabeth who was one of the secretaries.

"It's these blasted dahlias that have been swimming about in a vase of putrid green water and the act of leaving them here was perpetrated by a nameless person who is, as we speak, sunning herself in Ibiza," she announced in her perfectly received pronunciation.

She ran to get them as far away as possible just before The Minister arrived in the lift. Elizabeth went down in one lift as the Minister stepped out of the other. Standing waiting to greet her I put out my right hand to shake hers and put the dahlia problem to the back of my mind.

She was introduced to all the staff and the visit went really well. However when I finished filling my time sheet that evening I was not sure if I should list searching for a smell as an appropriate use of Civil Service time or whether that would blow the whole computer programme to smithereens.

That particular morning I carried the heavy clay pots around the corner and laid them one by one against the side of my large greenhouse. The wide spheres of pink, red and peach were set off by crisp, dark, pointed leaves and looked stunning. The greenhouse door was ever so slightly resistant and squeaked as I pulled it to one side. I never tired of the intoxicating scent of an autumn greenhouse.

The last of the fat, red tomatoes hung on to their vines with miraculous tenacity. I was just admiring my orchids, always best in the early morning light, when a shout from the window, shook me out of my reverie

"Mum, where is my rugby kit?" Another day here in paradise had begun.

The next hour passed in a recognisable blur and soon the four of us were on our way. Theo drove himself and Miranda to Sixth Form College and I dropped James off at school before heading to my office in town. As we drove up on to the main road James said "When is Dad back?"

Our lovely house was set in dappled woodland, with silver birch and conifers as far as the eye could see and I was just admiring them when he spoke to me.

"Not until Saturday morning, I am afraid, love," I replied.

The day passed, as days do, in a whirl of frenetic activity. I had a busy day with a delicious prawn sandwich for lunch at my desk. A large granary roll, fresh green salad and more large prawns than any person could really expect quivering in a delicious shiny pink sauce was only one of the delectable sandwiches available from a newly opened shop next door.

There was laughter as there always was, but lots of meetings and planning, as it was that time of year.

I liked to dress up for work but always swapped my high heels for trainers when I got to the car.

It was my particular anchor to remind me to leave work at the office. That evening I picked James up from his friend's house and headed home.

CHAPTER 13
The scent of lavender

The ache for home lives in all of us, the safe place where we can go and not be questioned.

Maya Angelou

I put my key in the lock as the hall clock chimed six. I stood for a moment and breathed in the scent of lavender polish. I remembered that Jean, the cleaning lady had been that day and would also have done the ironing… bliss.

My sense of domestic harmony lasted only a moment as I heard my sixteen year old daughter Miranda and seventeen year old son Theo yelling at each other about some television programme they were watching together.

I put my head round the door "Everything, Ok?" They both smiled at me and said in unison "What's for supper?" James threw his football kit in the laundry and went to join his siblings in the television room.

I meandered into the kitchen stopping at the fridge to extricate the lamb chops I had bought the day before. I poured myself a glass of cold water and took two pink Migralieve tablets out of the box. I had developed migraine in my early teens and these trusty tablets were the only thing that worked for me. My headache had been threatening all day and as I looked out on a golden autumn evening I wondered if we were going to have rain.

I was thirty seven years old and really enjoying my life. My family seemed settled; I loved my house and I had made a great group of friends since I started work. I also loved the fabulous social occasions that came with my husband's job. Trips abroad and being guest of honour at splendid functions was really exciting. We have been to fabulous hotels in Rome, Venice and Paris since he started this new job. I little thrill of anticipation ran through me.

I was still leaning on the sink daydreaming when I was surprised to feel my husband's welcome arms round my waist,

"Hello stranger," he whispered into my ear.

My knees went weak as I turned around. I was really delighted as he was not due home for a couple of days.

"I have to go back again tomorrow," he said, "but I just felt the need to see you all tonight".

"Shall we all go out for dinner," he suggested.

The children all declined his offer of dinner out as they all had homework so I cooked the chops and mashed potato for them and about nine pm Grant and I went out for a couple of hours. As I was getting ready a thought crossed my mind that he had come home to tell me something but I banished that. He loved his job and I could not see that he would want a change.

Anyway even if he did, he would have to get on with it as we had two children going to University in the next couple of years,

We sat and talked as we had our supper. I had a small green salad as I was obsessed with keeping slim at that time and he had a large rib eye steak. We walked home on the clearest night imaginable. It was warm and bright and eerily calm. It was the stillest night, without a breath of wind.

When we got home we walked around our lovely acre garden and I showed him the impatient plants that I had potted up that day.

"I will put those in the car for you in the morning before I go out," Grant said kindly.

As he unlocked the front door I looked up at the huge fir tree that stood about ten feet away from the twenty foot arched window that was a feature of the front of the house.

I had learned by then that whatever fate hands you in the outside world, you cope with as best you can and then you go home. This is your sanctuary, the place where you are safest in the whole of the universe.

CHAPTER 14
Things that go bump in the night

You must do the things you think you cannot do.
Eleanor Roosevelt

I was on my feet as though I had shot out of a cannon. Whatever the noise was it was cataclysmic. For some reason the first thought in my mind was that an aeroplane had crashed into the house.

I ran out of my bedroom and then bumped into my oldest son Theo on the landing. We stared at each other frozen with shock. Theo was now six foot three and very much a capable man. He held on to me as we rocked backwards and forwards in the turbulent, violent conditions. I have never been so scared either before or since. As the lightening flashed I looked over his shoulder, through his bedroom window, and realised that not only had my plants gone forever but so had my beloved greenhouse. Gone forever, disappeared into that raging night!

"What the hell is happening" I managed to scream.

Grant joined us on the landing and from our vantage point we realised that the tree had come through the house and had completely blocked the stairs. A hurricane storm had blown away everything in its path, flinging it wildly into the air. The three of us were being pressed against the walls by the menacing, gale force ferocity of the wind.

Grant made his way down the hallway inch by inch flattened against the wall by the ferocity of the wind and the pouring rain that was coming sideways and stinging everybody. He was going to get Miranda who could sleep through anything. Theo made his way after him to rescue James who was stood wild-eyed at his bedroom door.

The strength of the roaring storm pushed me violently back into the bedroom and I experienced a moment of sheer unbridled terror. It was the noise that was the worst, like the roar of a hundred jet engines. I forced my way back onto the landing looking for my precious family. I saw Theo first with his thirteen year old brother James hanging onto his back. He brushed forcefully past me and flung his brother on the bed.

He dashed back to look for his father and sister and I realised I was being peppered by thousands of little stones all over my body and face. We had a large gravelled driveway and the force of the wind was swirling the gravel in the air and sending it pell mell into the house through the open frontage. Myriad plants and muddy soil were following close behind like missiles in a raid. I felt faint and started to shake then I realised that I was holding my breath.

I let it go in relief, as I saw my husband, daughter and oldest son in a line, backs against the wall coming towards me step by step along the landing wall. I ran back to comfort my youngest son and when they reached the bedroom door they managed to push it closed behind them and barricade it with a chest of drawers

We scrabbled around in those drawers to find warm sweaters for everyone. We could not talk over the howling noise and then we realised that we could see flashes of lightening illuminating the darkness. We looked out through the windows and in the distance street lights were being blown over and arcs of light were sparking all around them.

I huddled my adult sized children to me as we made a plan. Grant and Theo decided that we were safest waiting in the bedroom until the storm abated.

That dark night proved endless but about two am Grant realised he had a small battery powered radio in his wardrobe. Once we were able listen to the news I felt calmer. The Weather Gods had obviously heard the bespectacled BBC forecaster Michael Fish say

"A lady has just rung in to say she had heard there was going to be a hurricane".

Then he uttered the fateful words that were going to haunt him for the rest of his life.

"Well if you are watching do not worry, there isn't!"

About six am the wind started to drop, Grant and Theo decided to see if they could get downstairs. They eventually climbed over the tree and shouted up that the animals in the kitchen were fine.

The kitchen was at the back of the house and was intact and so with help we made our way over the tree and into the kitchen. It was the first time in my life I had ever climbed a tree and the feeling of elation that that engendered was soon extinguished.

The rooms at the front of the house the sitting room, dining room, study and hall were open to the elements. It seemed to me that the whole of the front garden and the gravel drive had been dumped inside the house. There was no gas, no electric but we did have a primus stove in the laundry room and within five minutes we were drinking campfire tea.

CHAPTER 15
Dawn is breaking over there

In the midst of movement and chaos keep stillness inside of you .
Deepak Chopra

When dawn arrived the first thing the children wanted to do was drive around the neighbourhood and see what had happened. My heart was in my mouth but the three of them constituted too formal a deputation for me to argue against.

I was looking anxiously out of the dining room window when they pulled up back on to the drive. Actually to be truthful I was actually looking out of the hole where the front of the house should have been situated. They were full of stories of fallen trees and blocked roads but the most amazing news was that our house was actually the most damaged. We unfortunately had been at the centre of the wind tunnel. I could have lived without that particular accolade and thought mostly about how we were going to get through the next week!

I crunched across my beautiful new carpet in my wellington boots, through broken glass, mud and gravel. We had been told that it would be at least a week before the power supply was back on. Somehow the fact that all the food in the chess freezer was slowly melting as we spoke did not matter compared to fact that we were all alright.

The woodland around us was completely flattened in the storms of 1987. The tall firs were felled and the ubiquitous silver birches went down in their thousands. The fascinating thing was that within a year the new growth was high and within three years you could not see that there had ever been a problem. The saying that "nature abhors a vacuum" is very true.

We had all the extended family for Christmas and spent New Year at home. This was the last holiday that James would be satisfied watching television with his parents. He complained quietly to nobody in particular about the unfairness of being made to watch the adventures of Lt. Colombo with his elderly, thirty something, parents when everyone else was out and about.

Theo had gone into town with a group of friends and Miranda was at a house party in the next road. Not long afterwards the Columbo murder mystery had just started we heard the front doorbell ring. It was a group of Theo's friends that he had met up with in town and he had invited them all back to our house.

Grant let them in and I got up and retrieved some food out of the fridge and they stood in the dining room chatting and eating happily. Over the next hours as midnight approached the doorbell kept ringing with first one group of kids who we vaguely knew and then another arrived at our home.

Miranda came back and flung open the door and said very indignantly "Why didn't you tell me we were having a party?"

"We aren't, love." I replied exhaustedly.

"There must be fifty of Theo's friends in the kitchen and dining room" she said "Wherever is Theo?"

I would have liked to have an answer to that as I sang "Auld Lang Syne" with eclectic groups of cheerful teenagers and watched as they did the conger round my beautiful house and then demolished what was left in the cavernous fridge.

Theo never did come home that night. When I questioned him about the previous night's debacle he put his head on one side and said "Oh, yes I meant to come back for that."

I went to the study to speak to Grant and said "You need to step up here and speak to him about this behaviour" but he just smiled and said "Oh, it's alright he is young man, he's just having fun".

I tried to engage with Theo about how his behaviour had impacted on us but he just thought I was being a spoil sport. As he walked out of the room I thought to myself, "This is definitely the moment when he has become more powerful than the two of us put together and that fact will never change."

I should have done something about it then but then the thought drifted away as thoughts do when you are busy and preoccupied. I went to go out to buy the fixings for lunch again for the twelve guests we were expecting in two hours' time.

Not long afterwards was Theo's eighteenth birthday and we had a party for seventy of his friends at the local squash club. I did not know all the young people there as well as I had known all the children's friends in the Lakes. However they all seemed reasonable and well-mannered and I had met a lot of their parents. In actuality I found that evening very hard work as their behaviour was loud and increasingly raucous.

My slender, youthful thirty eight year old self suddenly realised with a start that evening that of course I was in no position to tell other people's eighteen to twenty five year olds that they could not drink alcohol!

Exactly twelve months later Miranda had her eighteenth birthday party at a lovely hotel in the same Suffolk town.

There were a hundred guests and it was an elegant affair filled with canapés, laughter and dancing until two a.m.

There are some definite differences between boys and girls behaviour at that age that you cannot fathom. The biggest one of course is that they are now men and women not boys and girls!

We had a lovely photograph taken that day just before we arrived for the party. The photographer stayed late in his studio for us and the photograph he took has always lived in the hallway of our house in whatever county or country that we have resided in.

A perfect reminder of a family unit before everyone starts to go their own way. The fact is when they next come back they will have girlfriends, boyfriends, fiancés, spouses and then best of all grandchildren with them and your family will just keep growing.

The family seemed to be doing well and my career was going from strength to strength. Grant's job meant he was very preoccupied but that was fine because I had made my own life in the two years we had lived in our new home.

I felt happy and I looked good as all that gardening had given me hip bones to die for and I had invested in a new vitamin K face cream that had helped my rosy complexion.

I very rarely got chance to watch television now but a new morning programme had been discussed in the office. Called *This Morning.* It was a magazine programme for women and the next morning I was home I watched it on Granada TV. I liked the presenters Richard and Judy as they really had chemistry and that turned out to be because they were a married couple.

A section about how to wash the dishes set my teeth on edge but on the whole I thought their style treated their audience at home as though they were sentient and perspicacious beings who liked to smile.

I thought there was a time and place for everything and daytime television could fill a gap in a long day for anyone who was home bound because of childcare responsibilities, redundancy, age or infirmity.

The Wright Stuff began to air in a morning on Channel Five and I occasionally caught a glimpse of the show and it appeared to me to be inclusive and slightly anarchic which I loved. Also I admired the way the host treated his guests with humour and intelligence whether they were men or women.

I wondered if this type of daytime television would catch on but as it would be a while before I was home more regularly the thought drifted from my consciousness.

Then the weekend arrived where one of my cousins invited us all to her wedding in Cheshire. Janine was ten years to the day younger than me and we had always been close. Her groom was an older man she had met at work and they seemed well suited in every respect.

The wedding was perfect in a tiny chapel in a pink hydrangea strewn wood. It was lovely to see all the extended family together again as the Canadian families were there too. The ceremony was lovely and the reception including lots of dancing and meeting new members of the family.

On my desk in a silver frame there is a photograph of the five of us together on that day, the children as tall as Grant and I and all smiling happily into the camera lens.

CHAPTER 16
Please don't make me do this again

Do not dwell on the past, do not dream of the future, concentrate the mind on the present moment.

Buddha

Grant had been away for a few days when I heard his car on the gravel drive and so I walked quickly to the front door discarding my flowered apron on the kitchen table. As I saw him closing the car door my heart froze and then sunk down and down into a whirl pool of pale grey trepidation.

He was carrying the most enormous bunch of flowers in his left hand. White lilies, lilac roses, green chrysanthemums and sweet smelling freesias tucked in here and there. I wondered what the greenery would be in such a hand crafted bouquet and a corner of my mind noticed the asparagus fern and pale grey eucalyptus.

After twenty odd years with this man I knew this could only mean life altering news.

Whilst drying my hands hastily on a matching tea towel I fixed a perfect smile on my face and stepping out on to the drive to greet him I leaned forward and kissed him.

"Have you had a good week?" I said brightly.

"I have news" he said quietly.

"I thought you might have" I said as I nodded towards the flowers and took them carefully from him with shaking hands.

"Shall we go inside,?" was his response as he began to walk towards the house.

"No, no. Please just tell me now," I said, "I cannot bear the suspense".

The anxiety was burning in his brown eyes turning them dark and unfathomable. I was leaning on the wall and glanced through the chink in the side door of the garage which was ajar. I spied the contents of my family's life.

A drum kit, cricket bats, bikes in every size, a freezer, a beer fridge, myriad school projects, pots of bulbs and that was just a snapshot of the treasure store within.

"I can't move all this again" I said and then my brain froze.

Of course my brain did not actually freeze; in the next particular metaphor my brain set of running like a hare being chased in circles with nowhere to hide. Fear crushed my solar plexus and was as real as a punch to the stomach.

My unconscious mind was telling me all I needed to know and I ignored it because I did not understand the signals it was sending me. When anyone looks back at their life there is usually a startling moment when they realise that if they had taken a different path that day, things would probably have been alright. The urge to do the right thing for my husband's career took over then and down that seductive path lay years of anguish and the loss of just about everything , but in my defence I did not know that then….

I wish my thirty something self, had known then what my older being knows now without question. You do not have to give an answer straight away and if you are forced to, then the answer always has to be no.

You must realise if you are saying yes to one thing you are always saying no to another, even if it's only peace of mind. You need to make sure you are financially secure in any relationship. Even with the best will in the world, he is only a man and cannot predict the future.

Stand right back and look carefully at the big picture.

Question yourself closely.

"If I do this thing what will happen and if I do the other thing what will happen then?"

However, unfortunately, I did not know then what I know now!

I could not take in what he was saying….. "Better job, they will rent us a house until we get settled……have to let them know tomorrow."

James was wandering round the garden with his treasured birthday present camera at that point, snapping away to his heart's content. Bella, our golden retriever was following him round the garden, her tail wagging, as she loved it when we were all home.

I slowly slid down the pale brick wall and there is a photo of me in high heeled shoes and a navy business suit, skirt hitched up, sitting crossed legged on the gravel with my head in my hands. My glossy dark hair, cut in a smart mid-length bob had fallen over my face and was hiding my expression.

Grant said he really wanted this new job and my wonderful children all agreed it would be alright with them. I lay awake at night with a feeling of foreboding in my solar plexus but I did not know how to stop a train that had already left the station.

I set off in a whirl of organisation. I was good at that as I had plenty of practice. My best friend at the office was the delightful and trustworthy Martin and he had often told me about the wonderful boarding school he had attended in his teens.

Set in the Surrey countryside the school was about ten miles from Grant's new office. There was to be travel with this new job and so we agreed that James would go to this excellent school, so he could board whilst we were away.

Theo had only had one more year at school before University but we could not organise the right mix of lessons for Theo anywhere, so both my older children would have to start sixth form again.

I fixed all the children's schools and got myself a new job within a couple of weeks. I was quite proud of my achievements as the six of us including our treasured golden retriever Bella piled into the car. We just left the house as it was; we turned the alarm on and slammed the door on our lives.

We went to the school outfitters in Guildford to get James' uniform. In this colourless "Are you being served?" environment he took the baggy grey trousers and a brown tweed jacket to try on. The fitting room was a corner of the old fashioned shop with a curtain across.

My embarrassed thirteen year old did not want his mother anywhere near him. I was stood at the other side of the shop smiling wanly at the elderly assistant, when through the silent air rang out a shout, as unexpected as a shot.

My normally perfectly well-mannered thirteen year old yelled "Bloody Hell Mum, if you think I am wearing this lot you have got another think coming !"

CHAPTER 17
What have I done this time?
Little children, headache: big children, heartache.
Italian proverb

I should have known then it was a monumental mistake from the start. Within a heartbeat everybody had changed. The elegant rented house in Surrey was lovely but it was not mine. James was a day boy at boarding school but we had to drop him off at seven thirty in the morning and could not pick him up until nine pm when he had finished his prep. However he settled in quickly and seemed to grow up overnight.

Miranda absolutely hated her new formal girl's school and left within a month. She found herself a job in a bank, made herself new friends and soon settled into being a grown up. When she came in the evening from work though she went straight up to her bedroom to watch television and I knew she missed her friends.

There was some excitement at the bank where she worked, just after she started there. Miranda was fortunately at the dentist but the girl who taken her under her wing, Vanessa, was working behind the counter. A young man came in with a gun and demanded all the money in the bank. Wearing a mask he spoke sharply to the cashier next to Vanessa who immediately complied with his wishes. Vanessa said she heard a voice from nowhere say " Would you like my money as well?" and then was horrified when she realised it was her that had spoken. Thankfully nobody was hurt but it did make the national press and caused a bit of a kerfuffle in the neighbourhood.

I did however wonder about the safety of this mythical place we called "A better life."

Theo on the other hand lasted six weeks at his new school. I came home from work one day to find him packing a bag and leaving me a note to say he was going back to live in the Lakes.

Knowing I could not dissuade him because of the glowering mood he was in and I ran to get some money for him out of the bank and drove him to the station.

I thought that a couple of weeks with his friends might be just what he needed to clear his head. We spoke most days and after about three weeks I asked him when he was coming home. "I am not actually" he said.

His friend Jonathan's father has given him a job.

It was the time of year when the vibrant orange tangerines were in the shops. I had popped to Marks and Spencer to get something for our supper and faced with a display of my oldest son's favourite fruit I began to cry and thought my heart would break. I wondered how I could have failed him so.

I did what I always did when feeling stressed I craved sugar. Along with plaice, broccoli and a bag of salad I bought a big bag of caramel popcorn. I opened it with my teeth and one hand whilst negotiating my way out of the gloomy car park with the other hand and the bag flew open as if it were a hand grenade.

My lovely woollen suit, my high heeled shoes and my hair were full of the sticky popcorn and it took me weeks to get it out of the car. Here we go again I thought, high farce is always the bedfellow of high drama in this category of up and downs that I call my life.

When Grant came home from work I was in tears. He thought for a moment and then said "I will leave in the morning; I have got to talk to him about his future".

Grant was gone for three days.

Father and son had driven to the North East coast and walked for miles on the beach discussing Theo's future. Grant begged him to come home and continue with his education but he refused and so he took him back to his friends in the Lake District.

Grant was visibly shaken when he got back to Surrey. "How can all this be worth it?" he said looking past me into the distance with tears in his eyes.

We also had Jake, a cheerful friend of Theo's from Suffolk staying with us. He had got a last minute place at one of the London Universities and could not find halls of residence. When Theo invited him to stay with us I said "Yes" on a temporary basis until he could make other arrangements.

When Theo left I had to ask him to find some student accommodation; it was breaking my heart to have him around now that my son had gone.

Of course I did not tell him this but said I thought it was time he settled nearer to his University anyway. He left a few days later to go and live with his sister who, unbeknown to me, actually lived about a mile from his place of study!

I came home a week later to find Theo back home and sitting in a chintz armchair more miserable than I had ever seen him before. I wanted to run and hug him but he was cold and prickly.

After a sleepless night I determined to do something about it that minute, it could not be beyond me. What could I do with a son who had eleven O levels but did not want to stay at his new school for his A levels. There had to be an answer.

That night I had a long conversation with my husband, and he said "Please do not ask me to do anymore, I have got my own career to think of and I need to keep my mind on what I am doing otherwise we will all be in trouble" Every fibre of his being seemed to be saying "Please leave me alone".

The next morning I rang my office and said I would not be in for a few days. There was a lot of huffing and puffing on the other end but I did not care if I never went to work again at that moment. I always worked very hard when I was there so hoped my private life interruptions would not count too much against me.

I tried hard to connect with my son that morning but I was struggling to find the words. I must have made forty phone calls about career choices and then I spoke to a really nice man at a local branch of a national company of surveyors.

"I am sure I can find something for him to do, bring him in now" he said.

Theo and I drove the four miles to the office and he had an interview with the nice man who said he had sons of his own. He employed Theo on the spot to train to as a surveyor and within a month he was off to Cyprus to help the company with a survey for a new airport on the Island.

He loved that job and spent a very happy year there He would ring me from all over the place including the top of St Paul's cathedral!

In one of those weird coincidences that life throws at you I actually met the wonderful man that employed Theo in a Budapest airport lounge many years later. We were travelling with the same chamber choir group and we just got chatting about our lives and the coincidence came to light.

I was able to thank him and tell him just how much he helped me at that difficult time in my life.

I had actually taken my new job in London as a stop gap until I could find the right career progression but in actual fact I loved the group of people I had gone to work with.

We were part of the press office and tasked with setting up a new department that involved solving problems from all over the British Isles. The first year I was there my life was going well and I was always out and about. My husband had a great job and every weekend we were off somewhere exciting and enjoying the corporate high life.

CHAPTER 18
The quivering omelette

Be content to remember that those who can make omelettes properly can do nothing else.

Hilaire Belloc

It was at this point that an unexpected piece of good fortune landed in our laps when a friend asked us if we would like to stay at their holiday cottage in Brittany the following week. We had visited there before as their guests but this time work commitments had stopped them taking up residence.

I rang my Mother and asked her if she and Father would like to join us for a few days. I was thrilled when she answered in the affirmative as I knew she usually hated surprises.

So began one of the most perfect weeks we had ever experienced.

The weather was crisp and clear as we boarded the ferry to cross the Channel. Mother seemed to relax more with every passing hour. The drive down to Brittany was easy and pleasant as Grant was a courteous and thoughtful driver who fitted in plenty of stops in the villages around the French Autoroutes. We expected delicious food from the start of our holiday and we were not disappointed.

Our very first lunch on the road consisted of soupe au pistou, warm French lentil salad with smoked sausage and a delicious tarte au citron. Relaxed and replete we completed our journey in good time.

Our friend's holiday cottage was in a tiny village and the garden was full of hollyhocks, lilies and bright blue scabious and the key as usual was under a small white stone by the back door.

As we opened the heavy, creaking back door Mother remarked that the place had a magical feel. As she was not given to whimsy I hoped this meant that she was really going to relax. The staircase rose unevenly from the corner of the kitchen and there was an old cream Aga near the window. Grant walked across to put the kettle on for a cup of tea and I took my parents up stairs to their bedroom.

The perfectly appointed room looked out over the stunning views. The bucolic scene stretched as far as the eye could see across rolling hills and verdant valleys.

Then Mother and I took a walk in the garden and to her delight when we checked the speckled brown hens she discovered that there were at least a dozen warm eggs waiting for us.

I watched my Mother collect the eggs with precision and economy of movement. She somehow looked as though she belonged in this rural scene. Her greying hair, cut elfin short shimmered in the sunlight and with her tanned, slender figure she looked lovely in her pale yellow sun dress. I thought at this moment the trick of the light made her look much younger than her early sixties.

Then I realised that it was because she looked happy and relaxed here in this garden.

I was a little surprised when she ventured into the chicken coup as I knew she was not that keen on animals. I was sitting on the bench under the fruit trees when she came to join me.

She laughed and said "Don't look so surprised. When I was a child in the thirties we always kept hens. The eggs were an integral part of our diet. I could do anything with them except wring their necks."

My hand fluttered to my mouth as I said, "Gosh Mum, why ever would anybody do that?"

"We had one for lunch on a Sunday of course. Grandfather Frank could dispatch a hen in one movement and Grandmother Hester could make at least three meals for a dozen people out of the bird. She made Sunday lunch, then chicken soup with dumplings and finally sandwiches for lunch boxes."

As we sat in the warm sunshine I thought about how little my Mother had ever looked backwards at her life, for her the future was what mattered. As we continued to stay there, with the drone of the bees in the background, I put my large, capable hand over her slender, elegant one for a moment and felt close to her and content.

It occurred to me then, that although I knew people in the countryside kept hens on their land, I had not realised that the poor in the 1930s crowded inner cities kept hens as well. With hindsight of course the city dwellers probably needed the eggs to supplement their diet more than the better fed country dwellers.

We wandered back into the kitchen and I found a large bowl and wooden spoon. Mother sat at the table and slowly began to crack and then stir the eggs whilst she sipped her tea.

Grant popped a nob of butter into an old frying pan and when salt and pepper had been added to Mother's satisfaction he tipped the resultant yellow nectar into the sizzling pan. He was known far and wide for his omelette prowess, snatching the pan off the heat at just the right moment with perfect precision.

I spent my time laying the table whilst Father sliced the still warm baguette we had picked up at the Boulangerie.

Soon we were outside sitting under the awning in the evening sunshine eating the delicious looking omelettes. They were crispy at the edges and glistening and quivering in the middle with a few garden herbs for garnish.

The scene must have looked perfect except for the fact that one of our party only ate one egg a year and she had eaten that at Easter. That person of course was me. Not wanting to spoil the scene I sipped my wine surreptitiously and slathered the yellow Normandy butter on copious amounts of warm bread whilst pushing the omelette round my plate.

After a lovely evening we headed to bed and I searched madly in my bag for an indigestion tablet before collapsing on the soft, enticing feather bed.

CHAPTER 19
The wild flower posy

And I will make thee beds of roses, and a thousand fragrant posies.
Christopher Marlowe

Each day passed slowly and luxuriously as we sat in the garden and read books or did the crossword. There is something especially bonding about four people trying to complete old copies of *The Times* crossword together. Many relaxed, convivial hours can go by as you sip your coffee and tax your brain in the most light hearted-manner.

One afternoon we decided to go for a stroll after lunch. Grant and my father Murray walked in front and my mother Mona and I walked more slowly behind.

The meadows we walked through were full of wild flowers of every hue and long whispering grasses and as we talked I kept bending down to pick flowers for her. I handed her each one so carefully and after a while I said "I bet you have a perfect posy by now."

I heard her laugh, that lovely tinkling sound she made when she was relaxed. "Oh gosh" she said "as you have been giving them to me I have been throwing them away, sorry."

We both laughed and agreed that she was not sentimental enough and I was far too sentimental for my own good. I am afraid that these were the days before we knew that we should leave wild flowers exactly where they were.

After a few perfect days we headed for Paris in the car. As we passed a street we knew I jumped out to go to a hotel that we had stayed in before. I started to explain in my haltering French that we needed two rooms but was met with an affirmative nod of the head

I ran back outside and after I waved the universal ok sign, they climbed out of the car to follow me inside. My parents had not been to Paris before so we took the Metro to the Champs de Mars station in the area around the Eiffel Tower and after a lovely stroll had a memorable meal. We each had steak frites followed by a sublime crème brulee and the men shared a bottle of Bordeaux.

We set of for the ferry the next day but before we left Paris we decided to drive along the Champs-Elyees. We could not believe our eyes as there was not a car anywhere and there were seats banked up on either side of the road. Grant suddenly said "What date is it?

As we all shouted "July 14th" at once we realised it was Bastille Day and that we must have been one of the last cars allowed through before the parade!

A sparkling few days to hold in the memory became especially poignant because I lost my darling Mother not long after that holiday.

CHAPTER 20
If I am injured do not send for my sister

A brother is a friend given by nature.
Jean Baptiste Legouve

My younger brother Harry was a very good rugby player and played competitively most of his life. One day when he was younger I came back from shopping and he was leaning over the bathroom sink moaning about his aches and pains in his shoulders. The bathroom door was ajar and I heard my solicitous voice enquire of him "Can I help you, Harry?"

"No thanks, love it's just the pains in my muscles as I have been playing rugby" he said.

"I know" I thought I have something in my bag for muscle pain. I searched about and from the depths of my Mary Poppins bag I produced my ancient, red Chinese decorated pot of Tiger Balm.

I had carried two pots around with me for years, the magic, bright green Zambuck and the fiery red Tiger Balm and I had never come across a malady that could not be cured by either one or the other.

I warmed a little in my hands and went back up to the bathroom where he was still leaning on the sink moaning. With little warning I began to rub Tiger Balm into his shoulders and said "This will make you feel…".

I did not finish my sentence as a terrible scream rent the air. "Get out, get out" he shouted trying to slam the door on me and get out of his jeans at the same time.

I heard him jump in the shower and then through gritted teeth he muttered "My back is full of cuts and abrasions from the scrum… you silly woman….. What agonising potion have you just rubbed into it?"

I did not hear anymore as I went downstairs to make a cup of tea. I rummaged in my bag and found a Crunchie for solace and was still eating that when he came downstairs.

"I am sorry I shouted at you" said my brother.

"I am so sorry I hurt you" I said.

He laughed as he continued "However in future I am going to carry a note that says

If I am injured do not under any circumstances send for my oldest sister."

This incident became a source of family hilarity and I could only say coldly that I was doing my best.

My Grandmother Hester had two sayings that she repeated with increasing regularity as she got older. One was "The road to hell is paved with good intentions" and I guess that this applied to the incident of "Harry's scrum shoulder".

Her other saying was "Sand Fairy Anne" and this was usually said with an insouciant shrug of her shoulders. As a child I used to wonder who Anne was and why she was a fairy on the beach. It was not until years later that I realised what she was actually saying was "Sans faire rein" meaning of course "It does not matter*"*

My youngest son James had a lot of sinus problems after we moved to East Anglia. My favoured form of treatment for this problem went back centuries and eschewed antibiotics.

"Boil a kettle and leave to cool a little before pouring the water in a heat proof bowl and adding trusty Vicks or the new-fangled Oil of Olbas. Put the patient's head over the bowl and completely cover both with a large white bath towel". James was always very patient with his mother despite knowing about Harry's rugby story and he actually usually required antibiotics for sinusitis anyway.

He was off from school one day with a headache and came to tell me to say his sinuses were blocked and painful. I was writing an article so for speed I said, "I know, we will do this inhalation with tap water".

I ran the hot water into the sink, which to be fair was very hot, and as it came out of the tap I threw in Vicks.

"There you go" I said and as he stepped forward I threw the requisite white bath sheet over his head, covering him and the sink in one swoop.

"Ouch, ouch, ouch, Mum", He yelled fighting to get out from under the large white John Lewis bath sheet that had enveloped his being. My son stood before me in his pyjama bottoms with his hair on end after the tussle with the towel.

I noticed two things, one was that his feet were doing a jig, a bit like River Dance and the other one was that he had a large red patch the shape of Australia on his chest. He was staring at me completely speechless.

Then I realised then that the towel I had thrown over him had dipped in the very hot water and landed on his chest and so had almost scalded him.

"Sorry, sorry, sorry, oh my goodness" I yelled as I ran downstairs.

Two seconds later I was back with the largest bag of frozen peas I could find and slapped it firmly on his chest.

We sat on the edge of the bath chatting whilst the heat dissipated from his chest and eventually he could see the funny side of it even if I couldn't.

He stood up and removed the by now soggy peas from his chest. This was harder than we imagined as the bag had melted slightly and stuck to his chest. He actually had a green *Birds Eyes Petit Pois* tattoo on his chest for several weeks.

He now carries a photocopy of his Uncle Harry's injury note only he has crossed, "Do not send for my sister" out to replace it with "Do not send for my mother under any circumstances!"

All I can say in my defence is that my good intention sense was very highly developed.

CHAPTER 21
I love this lake

Three things cannot be long hidden, the sun, the moon, the truth.
Buddha

I helped Grant organise that year's Oil Company conference in Montreux, Switzerland and it was just wonderful. From the moment we set off to the moment we got home it was perfect. If I ever have to visualise a place in my mind where I feel my very best, then it is always when I am standing on the shores of Lake Geneva looking across at Evian surrounded by spring flowers.

"I have on a beautiful white silk blouse and pink pearls in my ears and around my neck. I am standing tall in high heels and a beautiful black evening skirt. Looking out over Lake Geneva towards the Alps I can feel the sun on my head and the warm air dancing on my skin. I can hear desultory post prandial discussion all around me. Contented people are sharing snippets of conversation between them. I can feel a damp, chilled glass in my hand and have to tighten my grip slightly to stop the glass sliding away. I can smell coffee and the scent of new mown grass as the gardener chugs past me. In his wake I see beautiful spring flowers, tiny daffodils, hyacinths and muscari, blue as the Lake before me. I feel a hand on my arm and I am shaken out of my reverie…"

We had a perfect day on a glass train "The Alpine Express". Vintage trains that run through Gstaad have huge glass windows affording panoramic glimpses of some of the most spectacular views in the world. Quaint, alpine chalets cling on to the hillside with a perfect backdrop of snow-capped mountains. Connecting Interlaken with Montreux they serve the drinks on these trains in tilted glasses so that you do not spill a drop.

Lunch that day was cheese and more cheese in a perfect Alpine restaurant. The venue looked like a picture book version of a Swiss hostelry with panelled walls, bench seating and myriad cuckoo clocks that were all going off at different times. The menu was comprised of various versions of cheese and potato with a bit of bacon thrown in for good measure.

I mostly remember the sombre advice that the smiling, elderly waitress gave us that day as our food arrived. Her clear tones resonated around the room "Do not whatever you do eat hot melted cheese with cold beer. It will set like a stone in your stomach" Dozens of forks paused in mid-air as they were about to attack dishes of melted cheese in all its forms, Fondue, Raclette and my particular favourite, cheese and potatoes mixed together. The guests who did not have their folks poised to eat had long, cold glasses of beer to their lips ready to quench a major thirst.

Time stopped as we all looked at each other and an alarmingly loud "Cuckoo" ruptured the silence. First one person shrugged and then another and soon we were all eating molten cheese and drinking ice cold beer. The elderly lady was not seen again.

A member of our party suggested she may have been employed by the opposition to put the customers off this establishment and send them next door to theirs.

CHAPTER 22
Have we sold our house?

Don't let other people drive you crazy, when you know it's within walking distance.

Anonymous

As soon as we knew we were moving we put our house up for sale. The agent showed several people round and soon a middle aged couple from a town about twenty miles away made us a good offer. They were very keen and I actually met the chap one weekend when he was showing his builder round the house and garden. His mother-in-law was going to live with them and they were going to build an extension.

We had started going back home to East Anglia each weekend so that the children could see their friends. We left at lunchtime on Saturday when James had finished his rugby game and went back each Monday morning at five am so that we could all be at school and work on time. We also however, spent the occasional Saturday evening in A&E because James had either squashed his neck or banged his head whilst playing rugby.

I mentioned to him once that I was always relieved when the hockey season started and rugby finished. He gave me a strange look and said, "Mother, have you any idea how dangerous it is to play in goal in hockey?"

"Gosh," I thought, "Is that one more thing to worry about?"

We chose a charming old house about two miles from James school and looked forward to moving day. I began to get a little concerned when the contract signing day came and went but their solicitor convinced us it was alright and that we would exchange and complete on the same. We had moved house under those circumstances before and so it all sounded completely plausible.

To my chagrin the purchasing couple changed their minds on moving day.

"My wife does not want to leave her friends" the man said to our solicitor and we lost our lovely new house in Surrey.

Of course I felt concerned, but thought we would sell again quickly. It was just part of the game of snakes and ladders that was house moving.

That was except for the fact that their decision that fateful day was to absolutely change the trajectory for the rest of my life for ever.

I figured without Nigel Lawson and his plans for the economy. Up until that point you could get £30,000 tax relief on your mortgage. If two people who were not married bought a house then they got double tax relief £60,000. This decision to end that procedure had a catastrophic effect on house prices and our house along with everyone else's started to fall in value.

The trouble was that the fall in property prices our area was much more drastic than nearer to London and the gap in house prices became enormous. Not that it mattered because we could not sell our house for love nor money.

CHAPTER 23
They have rifled my knickers drawer

Every rascal is not a thief, but every thief is a rascal.
Aristotle

Life moved on and each weekend we played the same game of jumping in the car on Saturday lunchtime to go back to Suffolk to drive back at the crack of dawn on a Monday.

One summer's morning we all piled into the car at five am in Suffolk and then out of the car in Surrey at seven am to get ready to go our separate ways for the day. That particular day was a lovely sunny one and we had had a very pleasant journey that morning with everyone sharing their news.

Our rented house was large and double fronted and the dining room was the first window you could see in as you walked down the drive. Theo was standing leaning on the wall as I passed him. "My computer has gone," he said nodding towards the window and I let out a squeak of alarm.

Of course the front door was locked from the inside and we had to go round the back to see what had happened. The back door had been left wide open by the burglars.

Everything that belonged to us was gone. I looked round in alarm and began to shake.

Grant said, "I will get you a drink". He came back a moment later, "They have taken the booze".

Theo said "They have taken my leather jacket and the Tag Heuer watch you bought me for my birthday".

Miranda said "All my jewellery had gone".

We stood looking at each other. I went upstairs and realised all my underwear was thrown all over the bedroom.

When Grant came in I cried "They have rifled my knicker drawer."

He laughed and said "It could have been worse."

"How? " I screeched.

"You could have still been in them!" was his amused reply.

Just then James came running in "I have got a maths exam in an hour and they have stolen my blinking calculator.

Ten minutes later Grant was yelling through the letter box of WH Smiths in the shopping centre. The staff that were already in the shop were absolutely brilliant and soon pushed a calculator to him through the letterbox. Grant went back at nine am when the shop was open to pay for it and thank them.

The school holidays started that weekend and so Miranda, James and I all went back up North to visit my parents.

I sat at the kitchen table and for the first time admitted to my mother that I thought we had made a mistake moving south. She listened and nodded and then said "I am sure the family will have better opportunities in the South."

We had a perfect week with the family and had a trip around Tarn Hows which was our favourite place for a family walk. I went into my old office and exchanged news. It is a strange sensation to walk back into your previous life and see everything the same as it was before you left.

As luck would have it, a young friend Rosemary was in the office on her last trip back home. The youngest of four high achieving children she had suffered great angst about which way her life should go.

She had decided to enter a silent order of nuns in Rome and we had all wondered if it would be a success as she was such an effervescent personality. She had made the decision to continue and this was her last trip to see her parents. She looked exactly the same as I remembered her but as I hugged her I realised that there was something about her bright blue eyes that was now very different.

It was lovely to see all my friends and I must admit very strange to see a chap called Michael occupying the desk I had sat in for eight years. I suddenly had a flashback of the times. I had rushed in every morning to start a busy day and rushed out many afternoons to attend to attend to family incidences both major and minor. Those days sometimes felt like hard work, keeping all the balls in the air, but on reflection these had been some of the happiest days of my life.

When I was back in Surrey a few weeks later, I was waiting outside Marks and Spencer's food store for my daughter. We were expecting visitors for the weekend from France. I had been food shopping and my cart was full of heaving carrier bags of delicious food and wine. Miranda had rung from the bank to say she would help me to the car as it was after five pm.

Just as Miranda walked up to me smiling and waving a well-dressed elderly lady bent over and as she passed, picked up of two of my brimming carrier bags. As she walked off she said regally with an inclination of her perfectly coiffured head, "Thank you so much" and walked off with her bounty.

Miranda and I burst out laughing as she disappeared round the corner. We wondered about making an official report but as, in our surprise, neither could remember what she really looked like there seemed little point.

Further difficult news awaited me a couple of weeks later. My daughter, Miranda came into the kitchen and perched on the kitchen cabinet.

I waited with baited breath because I already had an idea what was on her mind and I knew she needed to talk.

"I cannot stay here in Surrey mum; I hate it I want to go back to my friends" she implored.

CHAPTER 24
I need to start my own life mum

Growing up is losing some illusions in order to acquire others.
Virginia Woolf

Miranda and I had got into the habit of doing fun things together and I was going to find it hard to bear if she moved out.

The week before a friend had a spare ticket for a Cliff Richard concert and she had come with me and my friends from work and laughed and danced all day. She made me promise not to tell her friends she had been to see him.

We met for lunch a lot and we went shopping together. However she was almost eighteen and I knew she had to get on with her own life. I still hoped she would change her mind and opt for University but that had to be her own choice in her own time.

I realised I was still staring at her and did not want her to know how much my heart was hurting. "Oh", I thought "oh what am I to do?" I took a deep breath and began to form the words in my mouth that were zipping around in my head like shooting stars.

"You can go on two conditions. One that you live in our house there and two that you find a friend who will stay with you." I conceded.

So began a really crazy period of my life. I worked four days in London and then rushed across town on a Thursday evening t to catch the train to spend three days with Miranda.

James was a weekly border so when he finished at weekend Grant brought him and Theo across to the other house.

It sounds like fun having two homes but I was exhausted and never knew where anything was. I was always reaching for something that was not there. The ketchup, a dress, a magazine or a bottle of wine were all elusive as each other.

Theo was travelling all over the country as a trainee surveyor. One week he was in Manchester the next in Edinburgh surveying whatever was the latest planned building or road.

I awoke every morning to the sound of Chris Tarrant and music on the radio. We had always listened to Radio Four but since we moved the sound of Capital Radio cheered my mornings.

One day not long after her move I had a phone call from Miranda.

"I enjoy my job and have worked for a little while, but Mum I need to finish my education" she said without preamble.

"That is wonderful love, I will talk to your Dad tonight" I said.

About a week later Theo rang me from where he was working in Manchester helping with the new underground system. I really did not like him doing this as to my ears it sounded quite dangerous with the trains whistling past.

"I really love surveying Mum but I need to finish my education".

"Brilliant love I will talk to your Dad tonight." I said.

They said that they did not plan it that way but that "great minds think alike!"

I was utterly delighted as guilt had been my constant companion since they finished school and I felt the worries of the world flutter off my shoulders like so many tiny blue butterflies.

When Grant came back from work we had a long chat. The decision was finally made that night, they both would have to go to a crammer to finish their A levels if they were going to get in University next year.

We decided to rent out the house in the woods that we could not sell because we needed the revenue and a pleasant army colonel and his family moved into our home.

Theo and Miranda went off to a crammer in Cambridge. They had the most amazing fun and met extraordinary people whilst they were there. In fact Theo met his future wife on the day he arrived and Miranda met the fascinating woman who was to become her daughter's godmother and lifelong friend.

A few months later they both had places at excellent universities and were beginning to have the time of their lives.

As I lay wide awake one night and I thought, with a frisson of self-satisfaction, "You see, there is more than one way up a mountain!"

Then we heard that the people who owned our London rented house were coming back from South Africa and I had to rush round and find us a new corporate rental. I asked Grant to help me and he just stared at me and shook his head.

A cold hand of fear grasped my heart but I just did what I always did. I pretended it was not happening and rushed about making plans.

CHAPTER 25
Is that a truck we are following?

Your pain is the breaking of the shell that encloses your understanding.
Khalil Gibran

I had been having occasional severe chest pains for a while and had just put them down to stress but after a time I had decided to see the doctor. After a careful examination he decided to send me to see a specialist. I rang the consultant's secretary and was given an appointment for ten pm the following Saturday night.

I stood in the dark outside the doctor's house and rang the doorbell. The drive was very steep and wooded and on his doorstep which tilted alarmingly, sat a large cage full of quails. I stared fascinated at the quails in the gloom and waited for someone to answer the door.

I started in surprise when I heard footsteps behind me but then I realised it was Grant, who had been parking the car.

"This is absolutely ridiculous" he muttered in a very cross voice. He thought it was private medicine gone mad when elderly consultants were seeing patients at this hour of the night.

He stood next to me tapping his foot. Eventually someone answered the door and I was ushered through to his office. The specialist was a bespectacled man well past retirement age who smiled at me from his chair behind a large mahogany desk. I looked round his office and saw amongst other things an exercise bike in the corner.

He peered at me over his glasses "Pains in chest and not yet forty." Let me see he said. "Right, take off your dress and bra and go and lie on the couch behind the curtain". I did as I was requested and lay there expecting to be examined. He whipped the curtain back with one fell swoop and proceeded to attach pads and wires to my voluptuous chest.

"On that exercise bike with you my girl and see how fast you can pedal!"

I stood up gingerly and padded across to the bike. Even though I am quite tall I only have short legs so it was definitely a bit of a kerfuffle to get on the high seat clad only in a pair of lime green Janet Reger knickers.

I had not expected to have my pants on show whilst he was examining my chest; otherwise I would have put something a little more Marks and Spencer on my bottom half.

I was pedalling away when I caught site of my reflection in the dark picture window.

My unleashed breasts were jiggling alarmingly as I was pedalling away as if I was in the Tour de France. I looked ridiculous but the doctor appeared to be taking his own time staring and making the diagnosis. I came to a juddering halt and he continued to stare at me.

He came quickly to a decision.

"You are doing too much, too much. Give up your job young woman and let your husband keep you. This is how life is meant to be!" he said with a jolly chuckle.

Grant did not ask me what the doctor had said as he slammed the car door loudly and started the engine.

A few weeks later we took James and our niece Claire up to Scotland for a holiday. We booked a forestry commission cabin in the Trossachs, a name that made me smile with delight every time I rolled it round my tongue.

The cabin was lovely but very rural and miles away from anything. There are so many things to do there like sailing, windsurfing and hill walking and wonderful restaurants abound. Scottish legends William Wallace and Rob Roy were both local lads and if you squinted ever so slightly on a misty day, you would swear you could see them coming over the hill. Local legend has it that this was the favourite holiday retreat of both Queen Victoria and Sir Walter Scott.

We had a walk the first day but the next morning I woke up at four am with chest pains.

"I feel really terrible" I said to my husband and with a deep, dramatic sigh he swung his feet on the floor and got out of bed.

We quickly rounded up the children and set off for the nearest hospital. We drove for miles, not speaking until we came to the outskirts of the nearest town, Stirling.

I could see the castle on the hill but we had no idea where the hospital was situated. Grant stopped the car in the dawn's milky light and waited by the side of the road. He waved to an oncoming driver and as he stopped he asked him about the nearest hospital.

The avuncular driver was kind and said "Follow me pal and I will have you there in no time".

I was actually escorted that morning, in the dawn's early light, to hospital by a very large rubbish truck with its full complement of attendant bin men.

As they pulled up they gave me a cheery wave as I staggered melodramatically inside. Two days later when Grant came to collect me the advice was the same "Slow down or you are going to make yourself very ill."

We spent the rest of the week taking it easy and eating the lovely food Scotland has to offer. Rich soups, delicious meat and fish dishes with lots of potatoes and puddings to die for.

We arrived home a week later and to my chagrin I realised I had put on a stone in weight.

CHAPTER 26
The big bear hug

He who has a why to live, can bear almost anything.
Frederick Nietzsche

A few weeks later Grant needed a small operation and James and I went up the hospital, which was forty miles away, with him. He was staying in overnight and James and I were booked into a local hotel. Whilst waiting for Grant to come out of the anaesthetic my chest pains started again.

I can almost hear my daughter saying "Always has to be about you, Mother!"

The chest pains got so bad I went outside and just lay on the grass. James went to get a nurse. She came out and looked at me with her hands on her hips.

"I know my love; I will get you some aspirin" she said after staring at me for some time. She very kindly did that and got me a drink of water as well. When the bill came I realised that I had been charged the princely sum of thirty seven pounds and fifty pence for the privilege.

My husband was fine, thank goodness but it was then I realised what a thoughtful man my youngest son was becoming. He took my arm and escorted me back to the hotel in the dark every night and made me feel that everything was going to be alright.

Of course what I did not know then and I do know now were that these chest pains were just part of the Multiple Sclerosis that I had been diagnosed with years before. They are called the MS Hug and make you feel like you are being squeezed in the middle by a very big bear.

Not that I had any experience of bears. My Aunt Amy's story always makes me laugh. When her children were small they lived near a canyon that had bears roaming around but they never came near the houses.

One misty British Columbia morning she got up to find a very large brown bear on its hind legs looking through her patio doors. She said "I ran to the curtains and shut them quickly, then I realised that the flowered cotton material would be no defence against a hungry bear".

She rounded her children up and went to her next door neighbour's house to ring the authorities. She laughed at herself when she told me the story because her first thought was if she could not see the bear, he would definitely forget about her.

CHAPTER 27
Wherever is my élan?

Thirty-five is a very attractive age: London society is full of women who have by their own choice remained 35 for years.

Oscar Wilde

Miranda helped me search for a new house to rent and eventually we found one. It was unfurnished so we arranged for some of our own furniture to come out of storage and we moved in. Grant had absolutely no interest and very rarely spoke when he was at home.

My fortieth birthday arrived and I had a simply perfect day. My children all came home and made me a lovely breakfast of French toast with maple syrup and strawberries. They gave me a delightful present between them, a beautiful butter soft, navy leather briefcase that I had been coveting in the village shop window.

When I got to the office there was cake and champagne and delightful presents and thirty of us went out for a special lunch at the local Italian restaurant. We were off to Ascot in the evening as our friends John and Jackie had invited us to join them at the races.

When we arrived at the Royal Berkshire Hotel a birthday party awaited me. A special dinner, gypsy violin music and lots of lovely presents were there for me. I loved every minute of it and felt very treasured by them.

As we walked back to the car park at two am I looked across at my husband and realised he had not even bought me a card. "There is definitely trouble in paradise," I thought.

To be honest I had so much fun, champagne and presents from other people that the thought disappeared like a will of the wisp to be examined another day.

Not long afterwards we were invited to a company event at Gleneagles. We arrived at the airport and I could tell at once there was something amiss. People would not meet my gaze and although they were still cordial something had changed. Grant was really distracted and cross with me when we were alone in the hotel room.

On one fateful day I found myself alone in the centre of Edinburgh sitting on a bench eating a big bag of delicious butter tablet from Thornton's. This ridiculous, sugar fuelled moment appeared to be the definite nadir of my fragile, contradictory existence.

My face actually hurt with the effort of trying to put a smile upon it.

Grant had left the hotel room early to play golf so I had gone on the designated rail trip with some of the other delegates. I went into Jenner's Department Store on Princes Street and to use up some of the solitary time, I had a makeup lesson. I bought a foundation brush and wondered what my mother would have thought about such unnecessary spending when I had perfectly good fingers!

As I waited for the party to assemble and get the train back to Gleneagles one of the older ladies sat next to me and patted my hand. I had been asked to give the ladies toast and thank you at the final formal dinner and as the piper finished his mournful tune and I stood up to speak I saw lots of sympathetic eyes resting on me.

Grant and I did not speak all the way home.

I had to face the fact that there was definitely something wrong with my husband. He was moody and distracted and would not engage with me in any way. One day he came home and just blurted out "I am going to work in Bristol, same company, same conditions. You will stay here and I will come home at weekends."

He refused to have any other discussion. I asked him if he was leaving me but he just stared at me with cold blood shot eyes. The people who rented our Suffolk home left the house as they had been posted to Cyprus. Grant worked at his new job in Bristol for six months but very rarely came home at weekends. I could not make my mind up what to do. Scared and overwhelmed by responsibility I just lived each day the best way I could.

I lay awake each night until the dawn's early light. Six am saw me walking Bella, our faithful golden retriever round by the stables and back through the woodland path where the bluebells grew in spring.

I really loved my job but I was also working freelance as well in London which boosted my income so I had to stay where I was for the time being. I had two children at University and one at an expensive private school. I could not give in to my feelings of anxiety.

Grant came home one evening months later and he said "I have been thinking, they want me to go to Cheltenham to run another company and I think you and the family should come as well". I felt so relieved and thought that perhaps our life would return to normal.

I explained to him that I thought the oldest children would not mind as they were at University in London but perhaps it was a good time for James to change schools.

I did what I always did, became so busy organising the logistics that I forgot to look at the big picture. I organised for James to attend a new school where he would be a weekly boarder, I went house hunting and then I found myself a job.

The best thing about being a civil servant was that you could work anywhere if there is a vacancy. I was interviewed for an amazing job at GCHQ and was really looking forward to starting a new career there.

The morning the letter arrived to say that I had got that really interesting job in Cheltenham my world collapsed.

CHAPTER 28
Please don't go to work today

I'm tired of being the girl who falls head over heels in love with a guy who barely even stumbles.

Anonymous

Grant was up early that morning and he was moping about in the kitchen "Don't go to work," he said ,"1 need to talk to you".

His sombre words and lack of the required bunch of flowers made me realise that this was indeed a very serious affair.

I rang the office to say I would be late and then came back to stare at him blankly. He would not meet my gaze and kept his head down. "Can we go for a walk?" he muttered standing half in and half out of the back door.

I went back up to the bedroom and put on my lipstick without looking, then rummaged about in my gym bag for my lace up, green flash trainers with shaking hands. As I stood up I caught site of my ashen face in the dressing table mirror and thought "Oh no, I wonder if he is going to leave me?"

I walked down stairs in my trainers and my work suit; I really had not got the energy to go back to get changed into something more suitable. Then I wondered to myself what the correct dress code for being dumped was.

We drove to Box Hill without speaking and walked slowly to the top of the hill each wrapped in our own misery and then stood, breathless, staring blindly at the amazing, misty view over the Surrey countryside.

"What is it?" I said resignedly

"I am bored and unhappy" he started.

"Give me a break, not this old story again," I thought quietly and then my head nearly exploded as he said, "and also I have to tell you I have quit my job."

I had absolutely not expected this in a million years.

"Oh my God, "I shouted as I burst into tears. "Are you mad? Do you know how many responsibilities we have? Two houses, two kids at University, James at that expensive school. I cannot do this on my own, you stupid, stupid fool"

Then I thought about my great new job. "Why aren't you going to Cheltenham? I have given my notice in London and I do not know what to do now".

I was crying red hot tears that landed heavily on my expensively silk clad bosom and I flicked them away with the hand that was not clutching my poor, aching head.

He looked at me for a brief second and then the shutters came back down.

"I am sick of moving, I want to do something different, I do not want this life with you" he said quietly.

"You, you do not want this life, you moron, what about me and my children" I yelled and with that jumped up and began to run back down the hill.

This action was obviously a big mistake, as it was so steep, that as I ran I stumbled, fell on my knees and then did a complete and extremely inelegant forward roll down the hill.

Even as I was busy falling I heard my grammar school gym mistress's voice in the back of my head say "Well done girl, that's the first time you have ever executed a perfect forward roll!"

I managed to right myself and sat for a minute on my bottom until the world stopped spinning.

"Maintain your dignity," I thought when I really felt like running back and shaking him.

"Try and get back to the car with as much self-control as you can muster." I whispered to myself.

When we got home I locked myself in the bathroom to think, think, think…… If I went back to live in our Suffolk house I could not earn enough money for us all to live. However, if I stayed where I was I could just about manage if I took on more private work and worked every weekend.

I stepped out of the bathroom and I could see he was lying on the bed. I would not meet his eyes as I was frightened of feeling sorry for him. No matter how cross and hurt I was, I still loved him.

"Are you depressed?" I asked calmly,

"Do you want to see the doctor again?" He shrugged his shoulders and shook his head slowly. He had suffered bouts of depression in his adult life and I wanted to be sure that this spell of unhappiness was not anything to do with that.

An important question next, "Is there going to be any money for us?"

"Some," he said.

"Are you going to look for another job?" I asked through gritted teeth and he shrugged again.

I set off walking to the station lost in my own thoughts. On the train I tried to make out my reflection in the grimy, smeared windows during the thirty minute journey, but it was an impossible task.

When I got to work I went to see my boss to see if could keep my job in her department.

When I sat down she looked up from her desk and burst out laughing. "Thanks for your fantastic support," I said and it sounded petulant even to my ears.

"Oh I am so sorry but just look at your knees" she chortled. I was startled to see that I still had my trainers on but more than that my tights were ripped to shreds and I had bright green knees where I had bounced along the grass. "Oh blast" I muttered inelegantly.

"Of course I want to keep you," Chris said. I ran round the desk and hugged her before going to look in a mirror before I met anyone else. When I looked I could hardly recognise the woman looking back at me.

I had a mad hairstyle full of grass and twigs where I had fallen. My face was red as a beetroot and thick black rivulets of mascara had run down my face where I had been crying and the set of my mouth was downward in a crazy misplaced smile.

"Get a grip young woman; you have people depending on you." I heard myself say. My high pitched voice shocked me as it resonated loudly around the grey, utilitarian ladies lavatory on the second floor of that old government building.

So I washed my face, put on my Ester Lauder peach lipstick (I was trying another shade) and yanked off my ruined tights and put them in the bin before I ran to get the train home again.

I studiously ignored anybody that waved at me.

On the train on the homeward journey I sat wrapped in my own misery but before long I was chuckling. A business man got on at the train at same station as me and very properly put his trilby, with the little green feather, and leather briefcase next to his folded suit jacket on the overhead rack. I had travelled on the same train with this chap before.

In a morning he put everything on the rack and then took out black leather gloves with which to read the *Daily Telegraph*. In the evening he repeated the same process using his gloves to read the *Evening Standard*.

The next stop as I was just sinking into my self-centred gloom when I heard a fracas down the carriage. A wild haired young man who looked like a student returning home with his washing had jumped on the train and slung his heavy bag on the rack, squashing Mr Telegraph's hat into eternity.

The absurdity of the ensuing argument made me smile and I reached home in slightly more improved spirits.

I rang James' school and smoothed everything over and when I told him he was very glad to be staying where he was.

Grant however had moved into the spare room and I could not get a word out of him however hard I tried. All I ever heard him say when he was bemoaning his life to himself was, "I am only forty three years old!"

CHAPTER 29
Self-indulgence is the name of the game

The Edge. There is no honest was to explain it, because the only people who really know where it is, are the ones that have gone over.

Hunter S. Thompson

As the weeks went by I knew he had lots of money because he had started spending with abandon but none of it was going in the joint account so I had no idea what was happening. My entreaties fell on deaf ears. I tried every resource I possessed to try to reach him. Kindness, anger, tears and guilt about the family made no difference. I even tried to hold him tight one night but his reserved and haughty demeanour made me realise that I was the last thing he wanted.

My own resources were dwindling fast as I had so many demands on them. I begged him to tell me what our financial situation was but when I started a conversation he just rushed out of the room shouting, holding his head in his hands.

The day before his sleek new company car was due to go back, he put his head round the door and said "I am off to look at a car". I thought "Oh good" as just assumed he meant a family car.

My parents arrived for a visit that day and I tried to keep a brave face whilst I talked to them about the family and my difficult situation. We had a nice lunch and talked of happier times.

At about three pm there was a loud noise on the drive, it sounded similar to the start of a Grand Prix to my ears.

My Mother, Father and I all went to stare out of the window.

Grant was sitting inside a bright yellow sports car with his Ray Ban sunglasses perched on the end of his nose. I was later to find out that he had given a large amount of money for the car without even having the engine checked.

The word cliché entered my head but that did not make it any less painful.

My mother's face was so downcast that I put my arm round her. She shook me off "I told you, I really did" she snapped at me as she went in the kitchen to make a cup of tea. I smiled because the only conversation we had ever had about Grant had been on the day before my wedding when out of the blue she had said "On your own head be it."

My parents were furious with my husband and left to go back North the next day.

Grant and I argued ferociously after they had gone and all he said was "It's my life, just leave me alone."

I said "You are forty three years old; do you intend to work again?"

"I have no idea" he replied

My father rang to say he had put a few hundred pounds in my bank to help me buy a car. I was so grateful but also deeply ashamed as this was the first time in my life I had ever needed help from my parents since I was sixteen years old. Whilst I was saying thank you to him in a phone call I felt my cheeks burning and hot tears of shame stinging my eyes.

So started a period of a few months where I rushed about like a mad women and Grant sat in a chair and stared at me. He would go off for a couple of days and I never, ever saw a penny of the money that he received from his company.

I got the impression everything was gone including all the stocks and shares.

We had been out together once in my car and he was driving. It was raining hard and as I began to speak to him he stopped, glared at me and got out of the car and walked away.

The cacophony of car horns behind me jolted me into action and as I ran round to get in the driver's seat I thought through my tears "This is no way for anybody to have to live".

I did not see him again for a week.

One Saturday morning he was in the kitchen when I got up and he said cheerily "Do you fancy coming for a walk?" My ridiculous heart missed a beat and I thought maybe it's all going to be OK.

We walked past the stables and towards the woods. As we passed a beautiful cob horse standing by the gate I turned to admire his golden beauty and pat him on the nose.

Grant walked on ahead with the dog and I had to rush to catch him up. As I came up behind him I heard the same old litany and my heart sank. "I am bored, I am only young, what has happened to my life, this is entirely your fault," were some of the nicer things he was saying. I carried on walking two steps behind him into the woods.

As we reached the fork in the woodland road where the very best jam blackberries always were, I lost my patience with his self-pity.

I carefully removed my antique platinum wedding band that I had worn every day since I was a teenager and rolled it around and around with my fingers.

The ring felt like a perfect symbol of my crushed hopes. I felt the weight of it in my hand and as I squeezed it tightly, it bit into my palm. My eyes were closed and hot unbridled salty tears trickled down from the corners of my eyes and brushed my parched lips as they fell.

Now, anyone who knows me will tell you that I am a completely hopeless shot. I have tried tennis, squash, and cricket and no matter what it is, I cannot throw for toffee. With my heart breaking and tiny, breathless, wracked sobs coming from my chest, my unbidden arm flew in the air and my precious, platinum wedding ring left my grasp.

I was having a moment of absolute self-pity when a terrible yell rang out like a shot in the air. "Christ, what have you done to me you crazy woman!"

I opened my eyes to see him twenty feet away jumping up and down and holding both hands to his head "You have permanently injured me! I feel dizzy, I am sure I am concussed". He shouted as he jumped about.

"I am so sorry, it was a complete accident" I whispered trying to contain my rising hysteria.

The next hour saw us scrabbling about in the brambles looking for my wedding ring .Our darling Golden Retriever Bella thought it was a wonderful game and helped all she could .However we could not find it and I have never worn a wedding ring since.

After we got home in silence, I told him that I was going into hospital the next day for a few days for some Multiple Sclerosis tests. I told him that I was booked in for an MRI scan and a dreaded lumbar puncture.

I was really going for the sympathy vote and hoped he would put his arms round me but it was not to be.

As I apologised once again and handed him two paracetamol tablets with a glass of iced water he looked past me into the distance.

CHAPTER 30
I need to get my head together

Some of us are becoming the men we wanted to marry.
Gloria Steinem

The next morning as I was packing my case for the hospital, he put his head round the door.

"I have just made a decision...... I am going to go back to live in the Suffolk house for a while to get myself together".

I was really at the end of my tether with him but I certainly did not want him to sort his problems out eighty miles away from me.

I thought carefully about my response before I answered. I had seen him confused and unhappy before but never for this long. Sublimating an urge to run and kick him I said in a sweet voice "Do you really feel you need to get away, darling?"

"Definitely" he replied not meeting my gaze.

"What is it, why can't you tell me what your problem feels like, maybe we can sort it out together?" He shrugged and did that shuffling thing with his feet that meant he was out of the room double quick. As he was leaving the room he looked up. "You must know that I love you but..." he stuttered.

"But what for goodness sake, I am not a mind reader". If I had been I would have saved myself a lot of heartache over the years.

Anger was hovering inside me and ready to take flight and soar but I damped it down quickly.

Then I replied calmly "OK but if you live there you must promise me that you will pay the mortgage for the house and the bills there because I cannot keep doing everything, I am so weary."

He agreed he would look for another job whilst he was there and left that day. I rang the clinic and cancelled my tests and went to work on the train.

I should have looked at the big picture then, at the reasons why a kind, loving man would behave in this way but I didn't because I was too busy burying my head in the sand.

I worked three jobs to keep the show on the road. The rent on the corporate house was high but now that Grant was paying the much smaller mortgage on the other house I could just about manage to pay the bills. He would not take my calls but I know the children spoke to him regularly.

I worried about him and thought maybe he had had a breakdown of some kind but I also wondered if this was a forever thing.

I cried myself to sleep most nights listening to the World Service. My friends at work were brilliant and helped me see the funny side of my situation. One day I noticed that my shoes were gone and my darling friend Nina had taken them off my feet, gone across to the cobblers, had them mended and then brought them back and put them on my feet again.

The glamorous, imperious woman who had arrived in their midst two years before had disappeared into the haze of anguish.

My friends and I laughed a lot and it provided salve for my broken heart. I started Weight Watchers and one of the young chaps Michael put a sign on my office door that said Nil by Mouth which made us all laugh.

However they really could not understand why I cared so much about my intractable, careless husband.

My private work doing pension talks for blue chip companies was the most lucrative, but I had to be on good form to do the job I was paid to do. I was also driving round the country running training courses for a new policy that was becoming law.

Most days saw me whizzing up and down the motorway somewhere or other. When I was too ill to drive one of the children took time out from their busy lives to drive me wherever I wanted to go.

I saw Grant on the train one day in London. I had no idea where had been or was going and he just stared straight through me as though we were strangers and ignored me completely when I spoke to him.

One day I was rushing up the steep steps at Vauxhall to go to the Fire Brigade headquarters to give a talk when my high heeled shoe fell off and clattered down stairs in amongst hoards of people.

"Don't worry Cinderella, I've got it" boomed a voice from the bottom of the steps. That kind man really had no idea how much he cheered me up that morning.

CHAPTER 31
We need to pull together

Happy is the son whose faith in his mother remains unchallenged.
Louisa May Alcott

My oldest son Theo came back to live at home for a while and he drove to University every day. He had obviously come back to make sure I was alright but I did not realise that at the time.

The most amazing thing about all this was the way the children all pulled together and worked for each other. Miranda lent Theo her car because she did not need it in London. Theo drove James to school in the morning so that I could start work early.

When I got home one evening the brothers were laughing. That morning Theo had driven the forty five minutes round the M25 to his first lecture. As he was parking the car he realised that his younger brother James was still in the car with him.

"Why the heck didn't you remind me to drop you off at school" he said in exasperation.

"I don't really know. I was just enjoying the drive", was his younger brother's answer.

We also laughed a lot through our difficulties. One Sunday morning Theo was standing half in and half out of the patio doors. His inside half was watching an absorbing cricket match and his outside half was throwing an old cricket ball for Bella the golden retriever.

Unknown to him I had wandered outside with a basket of washing and was stood minding my own business pegging towels out on the whirly gig that stood at the bottom of the garden.

My darling son absentmindedly threw the ball for the dog and hearing a mysterious thwack turned to find his mother lay flat out on the grass. The cricket ball had hit me right on the back of the head.

After solicitously making sure I was alright, the mirth finally exploded and the children all fell about laughing. I however had to sleep on my face for a week because of the bump on the back of my head.

CHAPTER 32
The money mail stand

Children learn to smile from their parents.
Shinichi Suzuki

My parents came from the Lake District down to visit us as they were taking James and his cousin Claire for lunch at the House of Commons. It was the time of year when the Daily Mail Ideal Home Show was on and I was working as an advisor on the Money Mail stand. It was something I had done every year and I loved it.

I was always really well paid for this and usually bought something interesting with money they paid me. This year though was different as I was struggling to keep everyone where they needed to be.

We usually had lots of famous people come and ask about their pensions as they were mostly self-employed. Nobody ever disappointed but it was not for the first time that I thought that on the whole stars seemed smaller in real life than they did on the television or films.

I was saying goodbye to one of the "Dad's Army" chaps when I saw Mother and Father coming towards me. They both looked tanned as they had been on holiday but there was something about the set of my mother's shoulders concerned me.

We went to have a delicious lunch but she hardly ate anything and I felt the first stirrings of worry frame my troubled heart.

The problem is when you are busy and stressed you process a particular mind set. The only way I could cope with what was happening to my life was to set my mind on an "eternal today" setting.

"There is no yesterday and no tomorrow, just an eternal today where I must do my very best. Most of all, this day must not end any worse than the morning started."

I repeated this mantra to myself every morning and so far it was getting us through.

CHAPTER 33
My difficult day

A woman is like a teabag, you can't tell how strong she is until you put her in hot water.   *Eleanor Roosevelt*

We were actually doing quite well all things considered. Money was very tight but the older children had taken part time jobs so we could just about manage. I had not heard anything from my husband but knew he was still living in our Suffolk home because I heard from former work colleagues that they had seen him around town.

I had even heard from a bemused colleague that Grant had been seen dancing in a night club and for some reason that made me roar with laughter even though the pain in my heart was suffocating me.

One morning I had a worried phone call from my father "Your mother is not well she has a bad earache and they have taken her into hospital. I rang my daughter at her London house and arranged to meet her at Euston station in London. I left the boys together at home and told them I would be a couple of days.

We got to up the Lakeland hospital in five hours and mother was sitting up in bed in her hand knitted pink bed jacket, even though she was attached to drips. We stayed a couple of days and she was reading the *Guardian* at the kitchen table, safely back at home when we left to get the train back to London.

Miranda went back to University in London and I went to my office. After about three hours I began to shake violently so I decided that I must have the flu and went home.

Theo's girlfriend Suzanne was at the house when I got home. They had been together since the first day they met at the sixth form crammer and were very close. She spent most of her time with us whilst she was at University in London.

That afternoon I went straight to bed and lay shaking, I just knew my mother was really poorly and I could not bear the thought that I was going to lose her. Suzanne came in to tell me a story about a phone call she had just had and her voice had a strange far away muffled quality.

The next morning my father rang again. "Your mother is back in hospital you need to come back."

I took James to school and arranged for him to board for a few days and set off back up North. I met my father at the hospital and he was shaking his head.

"The doctors have decided to take her to Preston Hospital and I want you to ride in the ambulance with her". She had on her woollen red dressing gown as it was a chilly April day.

Her severely cut silver hair framed her tiny face and her beautiful green eyes were tightly closed. I watched the countryside rushing by and thought my heart was going to break. We held hands all the way there and I realised that hers were decidedly chilly.

She had always made the most exquisite "cool hands" pastry. The most perfect sweet and savoury short crust, the ingredients measured out in precise detail and baked to perfection for exactly the right number of minutes.

However it was puff pastry that she excelled at making. When I was a child I would watch mesmerised as she carefully measured out the precise ingredients. Ice cold water, ice cold butter cut into tiny chunks, flour and the tiniest pinch of salt. The butter had to be spread out and the pastry folded and turned in the exact correct measurements.

She was so elegant, so precise and took ages to do everything properly. She could not deal with anything" slapdash" and I am afraid that was my middle name. I could make a cake with one hand whilst feeding a baby with another. I could dig a vegetable patch whilst studying for an cxam and I was always rushing about trying to pack as much in as I could.

That cut no ice with my mother as she was convinced that the longer you took to do something the better it was. She had a saying for her oldest daughter "You will meet yourself coming back my girl."

Her other two sayings for me were "On your own head be it" and "Keep your hand on your halfpenny" but that was about something else entirely.

Her eyes opened as we reached Preston Hospital and she squeezed my hand. I kissed her cool forehead and I told her that my father and Gillian and Harry were driving in the car behind and would be there soon. She whispered "I just want your father" and closed her eyes again.

My father's heart was breaking and in crisis he did what he did, he bossed his adult children around. We stood around Mother whilst they did all the tests. She seemed to be either in a deep sleep or unconscious when we left that night. She was wrapped in a silver foil blanket and as I was leaving the ward I started coughing and her clear voice rang out "Would someone get that girl a drink of water?" I realised that she could hear everything that had been said.

CHAPTER 34
Why can't we all go?

Woman hold up half the sky.
Mao Zedong

The next morning Father decided that only he and I would go to get Mother's test results. That left both my siblings, thirty something, professional people who were both parents themselves, standing holding hands on the drive as we drove off.

"Why can't we all go?" I asked as we drove off but he was brooking no discussion. He drove down the M6 at over a hundred miles an hour and we were there in a flash and my poor knees were knocking as we got out of the car.

We went to see Mother but she was asleep and so we kissed her gently and filed in to see the consultant. He was sitting behind his desk and he motioned us towards the two hospital chairs. One high backed easy chair which Father sat in and a utilitarian, hard seat that I perched on.

I leaned forward with my elbows on my knees and my hands holding up my chin. My spinning head seemed too heavy to hold up by itself and needed support.

In two short minutes we were back in the corridor and our lives were shattered into thousands of pieces. His words are etched on my brain, "Cancer in the brain I am afraid. It is a secondary but it is not worth looking for the primary site because I do not expect her to live more than forty eight hours".

He sighed then stood up, shook our hands and was off down the corridor. He seemed to be a kindly man with the worst of all jobs.

We went back to see her but there was no response and so we set off back up the motorway. We did not speak on the much slower journey home and when we got there he told my siblings in a very calm manner and then Father said "I am going for a walk, but you must all ring and tell her family"

The three of us held each other like we had not done since we were children. Then I looked at my watch and began to ring her siblings. Two of her sisters were in Canada and I cried when I told them as I knew they felt so far away.

We were having a cup of tea when my sister focused her eyes on me. She had been staring into the middle distance; we all were engaged in examining our own pain.

"Oh my love" she said "I do not know how to tell you this, so you need to go and look in the mirror".

The skin is the largest organ in the body and as such is vulnerable to stress. In the intervening three hours since the specialist had given us the news I had developed terrible psoriasis all over my body, except for the two round white spots where my elbows had been resting on my knees

I looked as though someone had poured boiling water over the whole of my body including my face. I barely glanced at myself and I thought "Now the outside really looks like the inside feels."

They rang us from the hospital to say they were bringing Mother back nearer to her home and she would be arriving there later on that day. We went across to the local hospital just as they were taking her out of the ambulance and her eyes were still closed.

My sister Gillian knew the ward sister who was called Jenny because she herself had worked at the hospital when her children were small.

Jenny said "I think we are going to put her in a private room so she can have some peace and quiet."

My exhausted mother who had not said a word for a couple of days piped up clearly "I hope you will not be expecting my credit card in return for this room as I do not agree with private medicine."

That was my darling mother, socialist to the end.

Jenny laughed and told her it was all part of the service and left us to it. Father marched us all into the corridor. "I do not whatever happens want her to know she is dying and I will brook no argument on this."

A noise in the doorway caught my attention and then shocked I said to him "What are you going to do about this lot then?"

Walking towards us were a dozen of her closest relatives, four of whom had just stepped off a nine hour flight from Vancouver.

There were lots of hugs and tears and then a plan was concocted by Father to make everyone agree to keep her prognosis to themselves.

Mother was as smart a whip and unsentimental to boot. She was known in the family as Miss Marple as she always ferretted out the truth, no matter what.

What she thought though as various people popped into see her as they "just happened to be passing" we never knew, because if we could keep the pretence up so could she.

After a week or so the doctor said we could take her home as you never knew a time line with these things.

Father made a bed up downstairs and with her comfortably ensconced in her own bed I set off home.

CHAPTER 35
What is going on here?

Love is like a puzzle. When you're in love all the pieces fit but when your heart
gets broken, it takes a while to get everything back together.

Anonymous

I got the train back down south and although I was covered from
head to toe in black, baggy trousers and a large white shirt my
face looked awfully strange. All I remember of that journey was
the terrible heat in the carriage. I picked up my car at the station and
went to get James from school and we went home.

He was due to be seventeen in a couple of months and had
grown alarmingly and was now a man. I knew he adored his
grandmother and was taking the news hard but it was difficult to find
the right words through my own pain. We had a nice supper and then
he said "I think I am better off boarding at school mum, I have exams
coming up and I need to concentrate.

Theo and Suzanne had already decided to get a flat nearer the
University as the travelling was getting too much and suddenly I was
on my own. For the very first time since I was about eleven years old
I had nobody to cook supper for but myself and so of course, I did not
bother.

Stuffing a block of chocolate into my dressing gown pocket I
climbed carefully up into the loft and got out the old record player. I
knew I needed to cry and the fastest way to do that was to put some of
my old vinyl records on the turntable.

I retrieved all my ancient albums including Scott Walker with
"No Regrets", Gerry Rafferty with *"Get it Right Next Time"*, Cliff
Richards with *"We Don't Talk Anymore"* as I knew any one of them
would do it.

The song that really sent me into free fall that night though was
"The Diary" by 1970s super group Bread.

I wailed like a banshee until the morning light found me asleep
on the dining room floor with my arms wrapped round one of my
husband's old sweaters, left behind in his rush to a new life.

Then I did what I always did in a crisis, I made a list. I decided that Grant had had enough time to find himself and I was going to make him talk to me later that day.

If James was going to board at school until he left for university then maybe it was time to go back to the house in Suffolk and see if I could get a job in my old office. I looked at the train times and realised I could still get into London most days to do my pension talks for private companies.

I had heard through the grapevine that Grant had been involved in setting up some kind of business and I thought now was the time to ask him to help me again with the family responsibilities.

I did finally find him to talk to but it was not the conciliatory discussion I had planned.

I decided to go into the office that day as I thought if I stayed in bed I would never get out of it again. I was also due to go to two different weddings of very dear friends that weekend.

When I got to my desk I realised my husband had left lots of messages. When I finally spoke to him the message was stark. "I am afraid I have sold the house and the contracts will be signed in about two weeks"

"You need my permission to do that and the house is full of my beautiful things" I sobbed "you need to give me a week to move everything".

He agreed he would and not for the first time I was running from the office with my head in my hands.

I got a taxi to the station and when the intercity train pulled in I got another taxi to complete my journey. It pulled up on the drive of my beautiful house and stared around. I had not been there for a while as Grant had asked me for some space to make his mind up and I had honoured that. My beautiful garden was overgrown and when I looked in the windows the house was empty.

I went through the heavy wooden back gate and sat gingerly on the swing under the apple tree. I realised then that I had made a big mistake letting him have so much space and time. It makes sense that when you are stressed and busy you do not have any physical time to do things. However the most damaging thing is that when you are really tired and anxious you cannot form rational, cogent thoughts.

That dangerous pathway is littered with errors of judgement and sometimes catastrophic mistakes. I had always known he was reckless and fickle but all this just defied explanation.

I really did not feel very well but in the days before mobile phones I was not sure how I was going to get out of the garden. I started to walk to the bus stop but my high heels were killing me on the bumpy country road.

I sat down on a wall to take them off when a woman I knew from the children's school stopped to speak to me. "Do you want a lift anywhere?" she said with a frown.

"The station would be great thanks, Jane" I said thankfully.

I got off the train at the station of the town where my bank account was held to see if they would let me borrow some money. The ridiculously young manager almost burst out laughing when I explained what I wanted.

He stroked his chin in a studied manner and pursed his lips so that a small whistle escaped.

"I did not expect him to have a wife like you…" he said under his breath

"I beg your pardon!" escaped from my chest like a bullet.

He shook his head…. "Actually I was just about to write to you" he said.

I was treated to a lecture about how having joint accounts with another person could be dangerous.

"Joint and several accounts and loans liability" was the basis of his haughty, wordy critique and I was outside again in the rain before I could say "Help me".

It turned out having a joint account with the man I loved meant I was much worse off than I thought.

CHAPTER 36
I have finally found you

When you give someone your whole heart and he does not want it, you cannot take it back. It's gone forever.

Sylvia Plath

I finally managed to get through to Grant that night after about a dozen abortive attempts. After all that had happened I am afraid I still adored him and really hoped he would find himself and come back to me.

"I hope this means you are coming home then?" was all I could manage.

"Gosh no" he said cheerily "I have already got a flat in town, in fact could I come back and get a few things like my desk and the rest of my clothes?"

We agreed that next Friday would be good as I was going up to the Lakes to see my mother. "Well ten out of ten for cheek" I thought as I put the phone down.

The girls at work thought I was mad to leave him alone in the house and so I was still there when he came on the next Friday. The first I heard was a furniture van on the drive and as he turned his key in the lock I got a little frisson of satisfaction over the shock on his face when he saw me standing there.

He came over and planted a kiss on my cheek.

He said solicitously "Hi, how are you?

It took every ounce of restraint I had from giving him a sharp kick on the shin.

It took him and the chap who had come to help him about two hours to put all his possessions into the van and as he pulled off the drive my future daughter-in-law Suzanne came round the corner. She was trying to make me feel better I know but I needed sometime to compose myself and wished that she would stop talking.

I am afraid I had done the worst thing possible by staying to see him because I realised with a sinking heart that I was as much in love with him as ever. When was I ever going to learn?

The teenage girl who had said to him "No matter what you do to me, I will always love you" had been prescient.

He had treated me appallingly and I was still madly in love with him and I knew I would take him back in a heartbeat. I knew that made me a fool that lacked self-esteem but that was just the way it was and I guessed always would be.

CHAPTER 37
She should know

Knitting and sewing mend the soul.
Anonymous

After Grant had got himself a flat I spent most weeks at work and most weekends three hundred and fifty miles away in the Lakes. My mother had rallied and was sitting up in bed knitting a complicated cable pattern that required three sharp needles.

Opinion was certainly varied at that point on whether Mother should be told about her imminent demise. Father insisted that she was not to be told under any circumstances and refused entry to the house for anyone he thought might give the game away. It was a small town and so the doctors and their wives were part of the social circle and I knew them well.

I spoke to Dr Jones and he was adamant that it was her right to know. I explained to him that she was smarter and more incisive than the rest of us put together and asked him to follow Father's lead and as he drove away he was shaking his head.

Dr Land came the next day and I spoke to him at length as well. He had looked after me during my last difficult pregnancy and had children the same age as mine. "I hear what you say and as the time is so short I will not say anything unless she asks me directly" was his reply. I assured him she wouldn't as I was convinced she knew exactly what was going on.

I met my sister-in-law Rebecca coming out of the house one day as I was going in. " This is not fair to your Mother" she said sharply " She deserves the chance to be able to put her affairs in order."

I looked at her blankly, "What affairs?" I asked. "Mother and Father shared everything. There is nothing to organise, what is hers is his."

I slowly took her hands in mine. "This is a ferociously private woman who will leave her worldly goods to her adored husband and take her thoughts and opinions to her grave." I offered gently.

I knew she loved Mother very much and was feeling very upset. I gave her a hug, straightened my mask to cheerful and walked through the French windows carrying the first of the gladioli that I had just found in the border.

I took the crystal vase from under the sink and arranged the cheerful lilac and purple spikes in a pleasing display. They did not look symmetrical so I ran out in the garden for some laurel leaves. A high hedge of laurel formed a perimeter to my parent's large garden and I thought nobody would miss a few carefully chosen leaves.

I stood for a moment thinking of happier times and my breath caught in my chest. Then I laughed out loud remembering the day that my father had admonished me for making holes in his lawn with my red shoes.

My preferred footwear for years, in good times and in bad, had been various brightly coloured high heels with peep toes, in the fashion of the forties. I could not bear shoes with closed fronts as for some crazy reason they made me feel claustrophobic.

Of course I could not convince Father that I had not been dancing on his perfect lawn, so apologised to him profusely. I had to smile a few hours later when he came to tell me that on closer inspection with his glasses on, under the cherry trees, he realised that the worms were responsible for the holes in his precious green swathe.

I added the laurel leaves to her favourite gladioli, made tea in her favourite china mugs, wiped away the tears that seemed always to be falling unbidden from my eyes and went to wake my sleeping Mother, as it was time for her medication. She opened her eyes and gave me a wonderful smile and said "I have just been for a walk in a wonderful garden where the sun was shining and the birds were singing."

Father who by now was stood beside me said "I think you are feeling better love."

She nodded and I gave a silent thanks to the universe for the machine that she was attached to that was pumping out enough opioids to keep the pain at bay.

I went back home to London to celebrate my daughter Miranda's twenty first birthday with her. She did not want any fuss as she and her older brother had big parties when they were eighteen so that seemed appropriate.

I booked the Italian restaurant next to my office in London where we had been many times before. Twenty close family and friends sat down to various Neapolitan dishes but our hearts were not in it and an hour later I was paying the bill as everyone trailed out into the warm summer evening.

Gino, the head chef, stood looking at the unfinished table with his arms outstretched in a question mark. "Sorry" I said "we are just all too sad to eat."

As I was reaching in bag for my car keys he gave me a big hug and patted my back in a fond farewell. As I looked in my handbag for my car keys I looked around at this familiar restaurant and wondered how my life had become so difficult. I was forty two years old and I felt as if another person inhabited this form. I reached out to touch the face I could see reflected in the mirror and was shocked when I saw how unhappy I looked.

I decided that it was really unfair of me to look so glum as we were all feeling the pain. I took a shuddering deep breath then straightened my hair and turned my frown upside down and walked outside into the balmy May evening.

I checked everybody was alright and after a sleepless night in my own bed, the next morning saw me at Euston station boarding the train back up North again.

CHAPTER 38
Up and down the country

What the daughter does, the mother did.
Anonymous

At the end of June I was back home again and rang to ask Grant if he would come back to Surrey to stay with James, as he was home for the summer holidays.

I wanted to go and spend what would turn out to be the last weeks of her life with the mother I adored so much.

He agreed to come and I set off up North to be with her. We had a lot of fun and laughter in those last few weeks of her life. The lines of worry and stress about the state of the world had disappeared and she looked calm and relaxed.

She had stopped reading the newspaper as she could not concentrate but loved watching the satirical new quiz *Have I got News for You* on television. She was on good form, constantly writing letters to all her sisters and nieces.

We had one incident of note in this peaceful oasis. Like many women of her age who were teenagers in the war my mother had always been a smoker. Always the same number of cigarettes, never amounting to twenty, always at the same time of day.

I never had attempted this frankly ridiculous pastime, as I could not get my head around putting something in your mouth and then setting fire to it!

My sister had been a social smoker at University and occasionally joined Mother in a cigarette if they were having a coffee together.

My mother's sister Aunt Beth was very proper on every level and passionately disagreed with smoking on every level.

She lived about fifty miles away from her sister and very rarely made an unannounced visit. This particular day Father was at his allotment and Gillian and Mother were sitting chatting and having a convivial cigarette. Mother was sitting up in bed and Gillian was in the chair opposite her.

I had just brought them both a cup of tea when Aunt Beth's smiling face appeared in the doorway. She took one look at my headmistress sister Gillian and began an incessant tirade of vitriol in her trademark high pitched, received pronunciation.

The fact that Aunt Beth was well under five feet tall only added to the drama of the occasion.

"You dreadful, thoughtless girl", she vented as her head and out stretched finger shook alarmingly, "how dare you smoke in front of an invalid?" and so it went on.

My broken hearted sister flew out of the room in floods of tears and I was turning to run after when I caught the look on my mother's face.

Our poor mother had hurriedly put her cigarette under the bedclothes in panic to hide it from her younger, but more vociferous sister.

As I stared at the carefully made bedclothes I could see plumes of white smoke coming from under the pale pink eiderdown and billowing about her person.

The air of palpable panic in that sunny sitting room that had been converted into a bed room affected me as well and I found myself screeching "Oh, Aunt Beth I need your advice in the kitchen."

She leapt up eagerly as there was nothing more she liked than giving advice to anyone that would listen.

As she followed me in the kitchen I said lamely, "Do you think we would be better with chicken or ham salad for lunch?"

I could hear the peals of laughter from the sitting room as Eric, Aunt Beth's husband, helped my mother extinguish the offending cigarette.

Aunt Beth decided on chicken salad and began to peel the tomatoes. I excused myself and went out to see my poor sister who was sitting in her car.

My darling, little sister was crying bitter tears and regaling against the universe, particularly Bossy Beth as she called her. "Why is this happening to us" she kept saying, "Mum is only in her sixties. For goodness sake she was in Cuba a few weeks ago."

I did not try to console her as she needed to cry and an ancient pale blue Volkswagen Beetle was as good a place as any on a sunny Lakeland day.

We all sat and ate lunch around Mother's bed and Uncle Eric made us all laugh, as he had since we were children. His jet black hair had turned into the most amazing silver mane and the only other person I had seen with hair like that was his sister Gwen.

Gwen happened to be my mother-in-law Laura's best friend. Gwen's husband had been a solicitor and both her children had followed him into the profession.

Gwen and Laura really enjoyed each other's company and a shared dislike of my poor Aunt Beth's haughty manner was a constant talking point when they ran out of desultory conversation, on their many holidays together.

They loved their Sheerings coach holidays as they considered them to be a cut above the rest. The fact that the two widows could stay in beautiful hotels without having to worry about their luggage and their personal safety meant they could travel with impunity until their eighties.

CHAPTER 39
A trip to Harley street

The art of medicine consists in amusing the patient while nature cures the disease.

Voltaire

A few days later an appointment came through for me to see a specialist in Harley Street. My skin was getting much worse and Mother wanted to know what was making me feel so bad that this had happened to me. Like every mother all over the world if your child has a problem you blame yourself.

She blamed herself for my psoriasis and no matter how many times I said,"You pass your eye colour, brains and foibles on to your kids, you do not get a choice in the matter," I knew she felt bad.

She insisted I kept my appointment and said she would be fine and I replied that I would be back in a day or so.

I jumped on the train and fell fast asleep. Four hours later I was back in the busy streets of London. I decided to take the very hot tube instead of a tax was a mistake but eventually I made my way across London to Harley Street.

I waited a while in his consulting rooms and then was called forward by a nurse that looked just like Hattie Jacques in Carry on Matron. She was obviously in awe of her employer and practically bowed as she went out of the room backwards.

I looked at the man peering at me over his glasses and wondered how I was going to keep an air of dignity whilst showing him my beleaguered body. Of course the answer was that I wasn't and as I looked up at him dressed only in my Marks and Spencer pants I wished I was a butterfly that could fly away through the open window. I closed my eyes and concentrated on the birdsong and the sound of the London traffic as he turned me round in a comedy pirouette lifting first one leg and the other.

As I opened my eyes he was staring straight at me with a silver implement in his small, liver spotted hand. "Open your mouth" he instructed. I did as asked. "Have you had a sore throat?"

"Yes, for about a month" I answered.

"Ha!" he said "A combination of streptococcus and stress, has caused this sorry mess"

He allowed himself his first wan smile as he said "Oh, I am a poet as well as a doctor."

Then as he put his serious face back on and I put my clothes back on he spoke to me.

"You need to be hospitalised for about two weeks" he said to me with his navy bow tie quivering "this is getting too bad to treat yourself."

I stared into his watery pale eyes and thought about what this would mean for my plans.

I wandered out of his Harley Street rooms and went to the John Lewis Department store to decide what to do. I had a cheese sandwich, even though I was trying to keep off bread and a pot of mint tea to help with the indigestion I knew the cheese sandwich was going to bestow on me.

I remembered my Father's words about other people's troubles being worse than your own and went to buy some pyjamas and a toothbrush as I had left my overnight bag on the train.

CHAPTER 40
The dratted egg salad

A diet is the penalty we pay for exceeding the feed limit.
Anonymous

The doctor had made a reservation for me at the Civil Service hospital in Kent and after talking it over with father on the phone I got the train down there on my own.

Rushing past the green and pleasant land that is the Garden of England, a sense of peace began to wash over me. I had loved the television programme *The Darling Buds of May* that ran between 1991 and 1993 with David Jason and Pam Ferris.

The title of the series made me think about Shakespeare's Sonnet eighteen.

Shall I compere thee to a summer's day?
Thou art more lovely and more temperate,
Rough winds do shake the darling buds of May,
And Summers lease hath all too short a date"
Sometimes too hot the eye of heaven shines
And often his gold complexion dimmed
And every fair from sometimes fair declines
By chance or natures changing course untrimmed,
But thy eternal summer should not fade.
Nor lose possession of that fair thou ow'st,
Nor shall death brag thou wander'st in his shade,
When in eternal lines to time thou grow'st.
So long as men can breathe, or eyes can see,
So long lives this and this gives life to thee.

The stories by H.E. Bates were salve for the soul. The tales of Ma and Pop Larkin and their brood of boisterous children were set in the 1950s.Its bucolic charm and wonderful scenery made us all yearn for a gentler time and launched the career of Catherine Zeta Jones as Mariette the oldest daughter.

The train lurched to a stop at my station and shook me out of my poetic reverie. An ancient taxi was waiting for me at the station to take me the last few miles to my destination

I was greeted with a smile and very quickly was sitting in my striped pyjamas on a plush pink chair that itched the back of my legs ever so slightly. Very soon I became calmer than I had felt for a while. When I think about it they must have given me some kind of medication to reduce the stress I was under.

I seemed to be the only patient in this hospital that seemed to be a throw back from the 1950s.Calm and quiet with lovely rooms with French windows that led out on to a wrought iron veranda.

My newly developed sense of peace and calm did not stop me getting a little hot under the collar with the first doctor who came to speak to me.

I had been measured and weighed when I arrived so I knew I was five foot seven inches tall and eleven stone two pounds. I thought that sounded fine until he announced with a sickly smile "Some women of your age are a little heavy and so we are putting you on our weight loss diet, as in our professional opinion, you need to lose a few pounds."

"Yummy, what a good idea" I remarked as he was followed by a lady in a pink uniform and starched hat carrying a dratted egg salad aloft as though it was the Koh i Noor diamond.

Later on a kindly nurse came to help me with all the treatment I needed and as she worked away we discussed the meaning of life. Her mother had just passed away and so was able to talk about how she felt about the loss.

A rather brusque nurse came the next day and flinging the covers back and staring at my ravaged body, she actually said "Oh my goodness me, no! Whatever does your husband think about this?"

I closed my eyes and did not open them until she left the room but I could feel hot tears squeezing from the corners of my eyes.

Spending the time walking alone in the delightful grounds was just what I needed. This time of year the pearliest of peonies were out in all the glory and their fat pink buds and bright green leaves provided solace for my breaking heart.

CHAPTER 41
Whoever is making that noise?

A heart breaking is not always as loud as a bomb exploding, sometimes it is a quiet as a feather falling. And the most painful thing is no-one hears it except you.

Author Unknown

Those hazy days developed a pattern of their own and I thought about all the other times I had been in hospital and how easy it was to get institutionalised very quickly. The rhythm of the day becomes the rhythm of you heart and as somebody else takes care of all your physical needs, a feeling of deep insouciance over takes you.

I felt calm and peaceful, the routine only broken by institutional watery salads of every variety. Their diet for larger ladies consisted of thinly sliced ham, egg and cheese served at every meal accompanied iceberg lettuce, cucumber and tasteless, woolly tomatoes   I did wonder how far that had to go to purchase such horrible, hard, pale green orbs, as the sun was beating down mercilessly in those endless tomato ripening July days.

I had been in the hospital for only four days when I woke up one morning with a start.

Hearing quick footsteps coming down the corridor I knew immediately who they belonged to after twenty odd years of listening to them.

I quickly sat up in bed because in the faint distance I could hear the most terrible wailing.

"My goodness" I thought "that poor person sounds as though they are in mortal agony".

Then I was having trouble breathing because a woollen jacket was being pressed against my sore, red face.

Suddenly I realised then that the person making the wailing sound was actually me, as the only reason my husband would have come to see me at five am in the morning was to tell me that my darling mother had died.

Suddenly it was all too much and I fainted clean away.

CHAPTER 42
The days went by in a haze

An ounce of Mother is worth a pound of clergy.
Spanish Proverb

When I came around again my bag was already packed and after a quick check over by the duty doctor I was allowed out of hospital.

Grant drove me straight up North without speaking another word. After shaking my father's hand and expressing his sorrow to him he turned on his heels and went back home to be with our children. He did not look at me as he left the house.

My father would not countenance my mother being on her own under any circumstances and so we spent the week in their house with the curtains closed and her coffin in the sitting room. Her sister Beth came and said kindly whilst holding my hand "At least she is with our dearest mother Hester now".

I patted her hand and thanked her for her kindness. I actually thought how little she knew her older sister, as I knew my mother thought all talk of the afterlife "A lot of ridiculous old tosh".

The days past in a haze and her two other sisters came back from Canada and stayed with us. One evening I was out in the garden at the side of the house when I started to cry and I felt someone's arms around me holding me very tight.

As I sobbed and sniffled I just assumed it was a cousin or an uncle holding me but when I stopped crying I looked up to realise that it was the Geoff the policeman from next door.

Although Mother liked his wife she never really warmed to him because he had been seconded to the picket lines in Yorkshire during the miner's strike. When I ventured that he had to go as it was his job she got cross with me for sticking up for him and that made me laugh which made her even crosser.

When I had calmed down I thanked Geoff for his kind act as it had meant a lot to me as I was feeling very alone.

Mother's funeral was to be on the Thursday and many people arrived for her service. She had lost her religious beliefs many years before. The Humanist service was conducted by a retired Methodist vicar and hit just the right note. The assembled cortege travelled slowly back to a local hotel for the requisite lunch and everyone stood around chatting inconsequentially to try and hide their broken hearts.

My mother-in-law Laura who was usually quite brusque said to me "I never knew a grown up girl who loved her mother as much as you loved yours".

I decided to take that as a compliment because she had known me since I was just fourteen.

I finally pinned my recalcitrant husband down and looked in his eyes. "You must have made your mind up by now, please tell me that you are coming home to me," I pleaded.

A stranger's cold dark eyes answered my question before I heard the sound of his voice "I will go back to Surrey with our youngest son James but once you are home, well… I am sorry I am never coming back to you"

Beyond humiliation I gasped, "Well, thank you for telling me today of all days; I would like to affirm that I am heartbroken but my poor, motherless soul is in smithereens and I cannot feel anything at all."

I hugged my children goodbye and gave James his birthday present as he was going to be seventeen the next day.

We waved them goodbye and I went back to the cold, empty house with my father.

CHAPTER 43
I am off to Oxfam

> A wise woman wishes to be no one's enemy: a wise woman refuses to be anyone's victim.
>
> *Maya Angelou*

The next morning Father leapt out of bed at six am and came into the bedroom to insist that we take all Mother's clothes and possessions to the Oxfam shop. She had supported Oxfam all her life and he thought they should have everything.

When I came around I agreed with this sentiment but begged him "Let's not do this on the day after her funeral".

That morning there was nothing I wanted to do less, as my body hurt so much. For me the dreaded, racking assault on the nerve endings that is arthritis comes hand in hand with psoriasis and I was in the middle of a massive flare up.

I rolled over and as my hand cast about on the pristine white duvet cover it made hollow patting sound. I was trying to find my ancient red Mulberry hand bag that I had put on the bed last night after looking at photographs of my children. When I did I managed to ferret out some painkillers to bring some relief for my hurting body I looked around for a glass of water.

Finding nothing resembling water I swigged them down with a gulp of last night's cold earl grey tea and then I began the process of facing the day.

My father stood over me as I struggled out of bed. He was beyond suffering after losing his wife of forty plus years and I had to help him get through this day.

When I stood in the cold north light of that cheerless bathroom I wondered why they never had the heating on. My mother had been so careful, even frugal, all her life with everything single thing and now all that doing without was over for her, forever.

Forcing myself to look in the mirror I noticed a rueful half smile was playing about my pursed lips and then I wondered why ever that was.

From childhood I had always been able to override my physical being with my mind, as I had been raised to never complain no matter what had happened.

"Count your blessings" was the mantra in our house. Woe betides anyone who broke the rule.

My father had always recounted his view on life "Ask everybody in your street to put their troubles down, take a good look at them all and you will be glad to pick your own up and take them back home"

Today as I stood shaking with cold and emotion I decided I was going to allow myself the luxury of counting my misfortunes and examine them one by one.

My father was already knocking on the door "Are you ready?" he enquired. His way of dealing with things is to keep busy and his rules were paramount.

"I need ten minutes to myself" I pleaded "Go and make a cup of tea, please."

I heard him sigh deeply and then the sound of his heavy footsteps echoed on the stairs and the kitchen door banged hard.

CHAPTER 44
I have cheekbones

I was lucky to be born with these cheekbones.
Suzy Parker

First of all I noticed that my knuckles had gone blue where I had been grasping the nineteen seventies avocado coloured sink. Blinking hard I finally managed to look up at the face that had served me so well, as a cheerfully arranged mask, all my life.

There was nothing but a bright red spectacle looking back at me. Even in my broken physical and mental state I noticed, with that spark of unconscious vanity that is hard wired in every woman's mind, that my cheekbones had reappeared.

I stared down at my slender legs, floppy stomach and drooping breasts and then noticed that there was no normal skin visible anywhere.

I stared back in the mirror anxious to divert my gaze from my body. My usually glossy dark hair looked frizzled and dry, like it belonged to somebody else.

"Oh Mum" I breathed in to that cold, empty space "Whatever am I going to do without you?"

My words landed gently on the mirror creating a small patch of welcome mist that partially obscured my image for a moment.

I took another deep breath as I tried unsuccessfully to run my fingers through my hair and so I searched for the utilitarian green shampoo.

A vision of my husband's handsome face entered my wretched mind,

"No wonder he does not want me, I would not want me" I said in anguish to myself.

The hot stinging water did what only water can do and refreshed my spirits as well as my body.

Ten minutes later I was in the kitchen wearing a loose cotton kaftan and my mother's bright pink Max Factor lipstick. I had plastered a smile on my face and that was how it was going to stay. "Just act as if everything is Ok" had been my childhood mantra and I was not going to let myself down.

Father had already started moving mother's clothes from her wardrobe and her top drawers contents were scattered all over her eiderdown.

To give myself time I went down to the kitchen and made some porridge for us both. As I stood giving the steaming, bubbling pan a desultory stir I wondered what to do next with the day.

My mind was completely empty but my heart was full of pain.

As I stood awkwardly at the kitchen sink I accidently put salt instead of sugar on my portion of the resultant grey gloop. I did not mind though because that careless punitive act perfectly suited my mental state.

CHAPTER 45
A lifetime wardrobe

All human beings are also dream beings, dreaming ties mankind together.

Jack Kerouac

At eight am I rang my headmistress sister Gillian and asked her for help with Father but she was due back at school that day and said she would call in later.

My mother had been so slim all her life even into middle age and as I looked through the slender contents of her jewellery box I felt like an intruder on her life. I decided to leave that painful task until I felt stronger.

Her actual wardrobe was a stylish 1970s wooden G Plan model, with two matching side portions with a dressing table and velour covered stool between them.

On one side of the wardrobe were her utilitarian slacks always purchased from Marks and Spencer's or Damart. Then I noticed her lavender padded hangers holding various turtle neck sweaters in pastel shades, flowered winceyette nighties and hand knitted cardigans with cable knit designs down the front.

In the back of the wardrobe was the star of the show, the ancient mink coat that had been passed down to her. It had been gifted from her Grandmother Hannah's mother, via her mother Hester and then to her, as the oldest daughter in the family.

She had only ever worn this for graduations, weddings and christenings as she was not quite sure where she stood on the animal welfare debate. Eventually she decided that as the coat had been purchased in the 1890s nobody would mind if she gave it the odd outing.

I buried my face in this exquisite old fashioned garment and inhaled the delicious scent of age old feminine elegance and beauty.

Joy by Jean Patou, the delicious combination of tuberose and jasmine flowers from the 1920s was Great Grandmother Hannah's favourite perfume. She applied this every day along with her uniform of smart brown gabardine suit and silk cream blouse held in place with a gorgeous antique cameo at the throat. She had been a hotel owner until her seventies and was never, ever glimpsed until she was appropriately turned out for the day.

It was Hannah who had taught me how to apply scent when I was about seven. "Take the precious bottle and after rolling it in your hands to release the vapours, spritz it in a swirling pattern in front of you. Then step smartly into the mist of fragrance which will cover your entire being."

CHAPTER 46
The Rose Perfume incident

A woman who does not wear perfume has no future.
Coco Chanel

As I stood there I remembered the incident of the rose perfume that had occurred when I got home from my East Anglian holiday with her as a six year old. I had gone straight into the garden I surreptitiously picked four of the largest deep red roses that I could see.

Running back into the wash house I separated the leaves and then bashed them with the end of rolling pin and put them in a cup of water. I looked at the sodden mass and wondered where to hide it as I knew mother would think it a ridiculous task.

Eventually I hid it on the highest shelf in the potting shed as I knew Murray my father only went in there on a Sunday.

I managed to keep stirring and hiding the contents for three weeks.

I knew there was a spare squeezey bottle under the kitchen sink. The only thing that usually got sprayed in our house was DDT at the flies.

The morning of the rose experiment results arrived and I took down the liquid in the cup and sniffed it. Well the rose scent had gone that was for sure and the colour was brown not red. "This must be what perfume is meant to be" I thought.

Sitting on the three legged stool in the shed I bit my bottom lip as I concentrated on pouring the precious liquid into the purloined plastic bottle. I thought through Hannah's instructions in my mind. The only trouble was that at six years old although I knew all my times tables backwards I had never come across the word spritz.

"I will just give it a go" I decided. Pumping blindly at the fly spray bottle I launched myself off the stool and into the mist.

Well blindly was the word as I did not remember there was also an instruction to "close ones eyes whilst running through the mist". As the terrible smell enveloped me and my eyes streamed painfully I had to go and confess all to my mother. She smiled a tight lipped smile while she stood throwing copious amounts of water onto my poor smarting, green eyes.

My Grandmother Hester always wore the fabulous Shocking by Schiaparelli, first released in 1937 with its similar floral notes, whenever she set off for her job at the Manchester Opera House.

Even after giving birth to eleven children I never saw her in anything that was not perfect styled. The ladies in the A la Modes shop over the bridge found clothes for her particularly and then visited her house to show her the collection personally. At a half an inch taller than her mother at four foot ten and a half everything for her had to be shortened and or let out. She wore a whalebone corset every day but all those pregnancies had taken their toll on her figure. She also wore very high heels every single day despite being a martyr to her corns.

My mother Mona had a bottle of Chanel No 5 on her bedside cabinet, that father had bought years ago and she kept for special occasions. This perfume is divine with notes of ylang-ylang, may rose and jasmine and she used it very sparingly. She had no interest in fuss and frippery and she most admired the politician Shirley Williams as a style icon.

Besides these three elegant and famous perfumes I also caught the faint scent of Lux soap and Ponds cold cream, an evocative mix from a childhood memory bank.

I forced myself back to the present and inhaled a deep, shuddering breath remembering these three remarkable women and the precious memories I had of them.

I realised that I had been sitting there for an hour and when I got up to look out of the window I saw my father speaking to a lady who was holding his hand in sadness for her lost neighbour.

CHAPTER 47
The dress parade

Say what you like about long dresses they cover a multitude of shins.
Mae West

When I had centred myself again, I took a peep in the other part of her wardrobe. The first thing I saw was the stiff, ancient white straw hat that Mother wore for weddings and a box of coloured silk flowers that she pinned on it alternately depending on her mood and her outfit.

Then as I swung the door all the way open the panoply of all the evening dresses she had ever made was standing in a row, like so many ladies waiting for their dance cards to be filled at a formal ball in nineteenth century Vienna.

The first one I lifted down was a 1960s deep green brocade dress with long sleeves and a pie crust collar. Each Christmas mother and father would go as guests of Lord and Lady Pilkington to the Pilkington Ball and mother always wore the same dress. When I asked her why she always wore the same dress she replied sagely "If the same dress each year is good enough for Lady Pilkington, it is good enough for me"

The next hand crafted number was a turquoise kaftan from the 1970s. This dress was floating and feminine and she wore it for her twenty fifth wedding anniversary. From the day of that party, I have a picture of her looking young and modern with her short blonde hair and a tan from her holiday in Devon.

Then there was my particular favourite. A cream lace fitted gown with puff sleeves and a handmade belt that showed off her tiny waist. I never remembered her wearing this to a formal function but it had been in her wardrobe since I was a child.

I put these on the silky pink eiderdown and ran my fingers along the rest of her handiwork feeling the weight of the different materials and thought about all the dinner dances she had been to with father. I knew that she had hated every single one. Almost completely deaf in one ear from childhood she had to be facing someone to get the full sense of what they were saying.

Intellectual and serious she found cocktail party chat vacuous and empty.

Her favourite thing in the world was to travel with her husband to his meeting in Bristol, Birmingham or Barrow in Furness and when he parked the car in a nearby road she would settle in with a red and green tartan blanket across her knees. The latest complicated jumper she was knitting, the *Guardian*, the new copy of *The New Statesman*, Radio Four and a quarter each of imperial mints and chewy bonbons were all she needed.

She would sit for many hours lost in a reverie that allowed only the loftiest of subjects to enter her space and time capsule.

CHAPTER 48
A ticket outside Oxfam

Sisters and Brothers are as close as hands and feet.
Vietnamese proverb

I sorted her treasured possessions carefully and divided them between her daughters and granddaughters. Her watches and ring would only fit my sister Gillian who had inherited mothers swan like neck and tiny wrists. I divided what was left including her pearls between the other members of her family including her sisters and daughter in law.

My day ended with a bump back down to reality with a parking ticket for remaining on the double yellow lines outside the charity shop.

Later that day I met my younger sister Gillian and brother Harry for a cup of coffee in town. We sat talking about the family and how things would be different from now on. We made a promise to each other that we would try to make sure that all the cousins remained close to each other.

As we headed for the car park I noticed our reflection in Williams and Glynn's bank window. I realised that the three of us were holding hands as we walked down the Market Place. I thought how in times of stress you are catapulted straight back into the arms of your original family members.

The next day I helped my father tidy the house and move the furniture around so that it would be comfortable when he arrived back to an empty home. I spent the afternoon cooking and filling the freezer so that he would have easy, nutritious meals to put in the microwave when he got back home.

I am a great believer that if you are in a good mood your food tastes delicious and if you are unhappy it shows up in your cuisine. I hoped this lot would not taste too bad. I felt as though I was trying to fill a giant chasm with a teaspoon but I had to start somewhere and this was as good a place as any other.

The following day father and I set off down south accompanied by my fifteen year old niece Claire. She agreed to come with us so that her granddad would not be alone on his journey back north.

Quiet and reserved she was very upset as she had been very close to her grandmother and me really appreciated her mature gesture of support.

CHAPTER 49
Who is driving the car?

As long as I am learning something I figure I'm OK-it's a decent day.
Hunter S. Thompson

After a five hour journey we arrived on the driveway I was perturbed to see that my car was gone. Grant had left that morning to go back to his flat as he knew I was arriving home some time that day. I put the key in the door and expected James to answer my cheery call but he was not at home.

Perturbed and anxious I looked around but thought he could not have gone far as Bella, the golden retriever was sitting in the kitchen. She was so excited to see me and ran around the house collecting any clothes, cushions or shoes that she could find. You always knew she was happy when she was sitting next to an eclectic mound of her families possessions and wagging her feathery tail vigorously.

Half an hour later the back door flew open and I was relieved to see my youngest son's smiling face. He was armed with the fixings for a delicious lunch. "I will just get the rest of the bags out of the car" he shouted as he disappeared back through the door.

I was after him like a bolt of lightning and stood with my arms folded like Mr Punch's wife Judy.

"What's going on?" I said to my seventeen years and four day old son. He laughed and put his free hand in his jeans back pocket. "My first licence inspection by the authorities" he said in a serious voice.

I looked at it then, "When did you pass you test?" I shrieked with my eyebrows firmly stuck about an inch from my hairline. "Yesterday" he said carelessly.

"It was a breeze!" then he disappeared into the house to prepare a delicious lunch for us all.

I knew he had been driving my small car around our gravel drive in Suffolk for years. I was so proud of him but never really got to the bottom of how he had learned to drive in four days

My teenage son and niece were a welcome distraction for Father that week and on Saturday James took his granddad to the cricket at The Oval whilst I went to a classical concert with Claire in Guildford. She was a gifted flute player and we both enjoyed the music that was balm to our souls that day.

On Sunday I waved my widowed father and niece off back up the motorway and wondered how he would cope alone.

About a month later James went to an eighteen birthday party in a dress suit and white trainers as was the fashion of the time. I took his photograph and as I knew he was staying at the country house where the party was being held I went to bed early.

At five am I heard him banging about downstairs and the next minute he was bouncing into the bedroom

"Come and look at this wonderful sunrise Mum, it's just amazing.

As I pulled my robe on and followed him barefoot on to the grass I realised he was quite correct.

"Life really is amazing."

PART TWO
CHAPTER 50
A night out with Margaret Rutherford

Rich foods shape our destiny, they too shape our ends.
Anonymous

I spent the next few months going up North to visit my widowed father when I had time off from work. He had made friends at the bridge club with a delightful lady called Dorothy who absolutely reminded me of Margaret Rutherford playing Miss Marple in *Murder Ahoy*!

One snowy evening we were going to see my oldest nephew Rufus as he had the lead in his school production of Peter Pan. He was quite an accomplished actor at this time as he spent every summer at the National Youth Theatre.

The evening before my sister Gillian had taken a party from the special school where she was the headmistress, to see her son in *Peter Pan*. As he got to the point where he had to say "I have no Mother" thirty voluble children decided to disagree with him.

"She's over here!" they were all shouting and complete order had to be restored before the play could go on.

That evening my Father, Dorothy and I were sitting near the front of the auditorium on the final evening of the show.

I had been on the ubiquitous cabbage soup diet for a few days as I was trying to lose weight again and the inevitable consequences of this noxious potion meant that I spent the entire evening wriggling, jiggling and gurgling,

"Please keep still" demanded my father.

For some reason I had ended up sitting between them on the row and I felt like a very naughty child and that made me want to giggle.

We all had a cup of tea in the school cafeteria as we had to wait for the star of the show to take his plaudits, then all four of us set off home.

Dorothy lived in a village about three miles from the school in a bungalow on a steeply sloping drive. We skidded to a stop outside her home and both Rufus and I got out helping Dorothy to try to get up the icy drive. This appeared to be impossible and eventually Father got out lending us a hand.

His presence made absolutely no difference until the lady next door came out in the snow to see what the commotion was about. It turned out to be Mavis, the French teacher from the other secondary school. I had known her for years and we exchanged pleasantries. She was a delightful woman with two lovely daughters and a perfect beehive that never, ever moved even when she was in her flowered winceyette pyjamas.

With an almighty effort she managed to pull as we pushed and eventually we got enough purchase to get Dorothy up to her front door.

As she wished us a wan goodnight my father already had the engine revving. I do not think they went on another date.

CHAPTER 51
The impacted wisdom teeth

There is never one sunset the same: or one sunrise the same.
Carlos Santana

As if I did not have enough to contend with, my wisdom teeth decided to put in an appearance and then they eventually became impacted.

I had an appointment at the hospital in London that just happened to be near my daughter's University. I had arranged to meet her for lunch and said I would wait in the University Car Park until she had finished her morning lectures.

The dental appointment did not take long and bored with waiting in the car I decided to go for a walk. The beautiful, warm spring day entranced me and I walked much further than I had intended.

The gardens were lovely, I could see two elderly gardeners standing chatting whilst they leaned on their spades. Perfectly tended verdant lawns set around the glorious cream, stone manor house that was at the heart of the campus.

As I walked I noticed the flowers and the planting arrangements and then I looked up. Without realising I had ended up near the lecture halls and when glanced up I saw one of Miranda's friends waving at me. She smiled and beckoned me over to her and stepping lightly on the verge I peered into the window. Sixty plus twenty year olds, most of whom I knew, were staring back at me.

Only two people did not laugh that day, the lecturer whose professorial flow had been interrupted and my red faced daughter whose mother had embarrassed her yet again.

I definitely needed surgery on my wisdom teeth and my oldest son Theo came to collect me from hospital the day after the operation. I was just waking up when I heard his voice and that of the nurse who had been looking after me. The conversation went as follows.

"I have come to collect my mother" said Theo.

"Oh gosh, yes" replied the young, obviously smitten nurse.

"She has had a bit of a reaction to the anaesthetic I am afraid , she keeps shouting for Richard in her sleep; does she know anybody called Richard?"

There was a moment's silence "No I don't think so," he replied

Then after another moment he said "Oh of course I know, it will be Cliff Richard, she is quite keen on him."

Then both their faces appeared in the doorway and had absolutely no idea why I was laughing helplessly after having several teeth painfully extracted.

CHAPTER 52
The Morris dancers

Dancing is like dreaming with your feet.
Constanze

About a month later I went up North again to see how my father was faring. He seemed more relaxed and settled so we decided to go to a May Festival in the town. The Festival was fun and I saw lots of people I knew from the office and the children's school. Everyone asked after Grant and I did not have the heart to say he had left me as if saying the words out loud would make it true.

We watched our previous neighbour Paul, who was the leader of the Morris Dancing troop getting ready to perform. He was six foot five in his stocking feet and looked very striking in his outfit and decorated hat: especially when he was with his social worker wife Janet who was only five feet tall. The Morris dancing dates back to the fifteenth century and is based upon rhythmic stepping.

The men normally wear white and carry short sticks or garlands. The dancers from the ancient county of Westmorland where we were wore clogs and danced in groups of eight accompanied by a band. Great fun was had by all that afternoon.

In the evening we walked out to what had been my favourite restaurant when I lived in the town. Trendy and serving vegetarian and slow cooked food full of garlic it had been the place to be seen. Father and I managed to get a corner table and discovered that a folk band was on that night and we joined in with the songs we knew.

As we walked home I realised that I had fun for the first time in ages and thought maybe I was finally moving on.

I spent the next day with my brother and sister and their families and enjoyed being with the children. As the sun shone that day I looked around and wondered why ever I had thought it was a good idea to move away from my happy existence here. I had everything I ever wanted in the life I had been living but it was too late now for regrets.

I had a real problem saying goodbye to them all as I rushed for the train back to London and my present predicament.

I could not concentrate on my Good Housekeeping magazine and spent most of the journey with my eyes closed so that nobody would engage me in conversation.

Wherever I was I usually enjoyed chatting with my travelling companions but on this particular journey considered that I would be a poor conversationalist.

CHAPTER 53
The Pirates of Penzance

The secret of staying young is to live honestly, eat slowly and lie about your age.

Lucille Ball

The time since Grant had left me had been really tough but I felt as though I was moving forward in my life.

Some days I practically skipped into the office but others were darker and fraught with difficulty. I caught horrible flu and stayed in bed for a week and did not see another soul the whole time. I cried a lot that week with abject self-pity, but was on my feet again soon afterwards with renewed vigour.

I lived near a stately home and some friends and colleagues had come to see a production of The Pirates of Penzance in which one of my friends had a starring role.

A woman of uncertain years named Sheila had just joined our office had a perfect, enviable figure.

Her motto was "Always walk when you have eaten, absolutely no exception!"

I made afternoon tea, before the show, for about twenty people and we were all deciding which cars to go in when with an elated wave Sheila set off on foot. Dressed up for the concert but with her trainers on she looked a little incongruous but it was her choice on that lovely summer's evening

I was not too concerned for her as it was only about a mile walk but as the first car of our convoy drove up the ancient house's long sweeping driveway, there she was, sitting on the grass. Being peered on by the flock of sheep that scattered the surrounding fields she was holding her bloodied and bashed nose.

She had tripped and fallen on her face and so with a smile I volunteered to miss the show and take her home.

We called back at my house for a bag of the ubiquitous frozen peas and we set off back into London. She was apologetic about the fact that I had missed the show but I assured her I already knew all the songs by heart. She firmly resisted my offer to give her a small rendition, as the resounding fall on her face had given her a headache.

On Monday she was back at work with the two blackest eyes I had ever seen. I felt so sorry for her and it just intensified my belief that no good ever comes of too much strenuous exercise.

She went to live in France a few weeks later so I never discovered whether she kept on walking every time she ate.

I had a little drinks party at home on my birthday and lots of friends came from work. When I caught sight of myself in the downstairs cloakroom mirror, I gave my shoulders a little shrug of insouciance and then executed a stylish twirl which might have been excitement or chardonnay, I do not really know.

CHAPTER 54
A holiday for twenty people

A holiday is like love, anticipated with pleasure, experienced with discomfort and remembered with nostalgia.

Anonymous

Mother had booked a holiday for all twenty of us in the family before her demise and Father insisted that she would have wanted us all still to go.

Honestly, I really did not want to go as I was working long hours but I realised that I was being churlish and so decided I should make the effort.

As I drove up in my car I saw a few of our party standing about chatting as they had not seen each other for a while. My solar plexus did a somersault as I recognised one of the people. My husband Grant was standing there smiling and chatting to the assembled company.

He had of course been invited the previous summer but I did not for a moment expect him to have the chutzpah to turn up.

He kissed my cheek and took my case as though he had only popped out for a loaf of bread instead of being away for a year.

I had never been to Centre Parks and to be honest did not know what to expect. Actually in reality we spent the week there as an extended family and lots of fun was had by everyone.

All the children's friends who lived locally arrived and spent the day with us and eventually we had enough people for two football teams.

My sister Gillian and I spent the week cycling and laughing whizzing through the woodland roads pretending that we were children again. We went for a facial and a massage and as we chatted she begged me to think carefully before I took Grant back, if he said he wanted to come home.

I looked at her and shrugged.

She started to speak slowly and carefully "I have known him since I was ten years old and I still do not understand why he is so unhappy. He is such a good man, I wish I knew,!" my poor sister exclaimed near to tears of frustration.

"I am getting by without him," I replied after a moment, "but I will always love him, more fool me."

After a week of swimming, playing tennis and general bonhomie we all said our farewells. It was such fun all to be together but our late Mother was never far from any of our thoughts.

As we were leaving, I put our golden retriever Bella in the car and I heard a familiar voice behind me.

"Is it alright if I come round for a chat this weekend," Grant remarked as he kissed me a fond adieu on both cheeks.

I voice that I did not recognise said compliantly "Fine, see you Sunday, then."

CHAPTER 55
The football team is in the lift

A civil servant does not make jokes.
Eugene Ionesco

My Civil Service office was on the second floor of the grey London office block that I worked in. My training rooms were on the twelfth floor and I was forever zipping up and down between the two places. Lots of interesting people worked in that building and I was on nodding terms with most of them.

School children dream of being an astronaut, a policeman or a teacher. However not many people leave school or university wanting to be a civil servant and the stories of how people had ended up doing their particular job were usually quite fascinating.

One particular sunny day I had just started a week long training course for about forty people.

Most new employees were young graduates but also some older people who had fancied a career change in midlife, women career returners and a general mixed group of mostly lovely people.

The term Civil Servant implied gravitas and security for anyone stuck with hard choices at a point in their life.

We got Oxbridge graduates who knowing everything about The Classics knew nothing about filing in alphabetical order.

We welcomed redundant Managing Directors who did not know that they had to buy their own train ticket or cup of coffee.

There were also clever recent graduates who could not find any employment prospects in their particular esoteric chosen subject.

Then there were women just like me who had tried to fit a working life around school hours, husband's careers and other responsibilities.

I loved this job as I felt I could relate to the majority of my new trainees and make the learning of a fairly dry subject matter interesting and occasionally amusing.

I introduced myself and as the morning wore on I developed a particularly awkward little cough. Water was not making any difference so I thought, "I know, I have a can of cola in my desk I will go and get that".

I gave the group some reading to be getting on with, excused myself and headed for the lifts. There was only Mr Singh, from the Pensions department and I together in the lift and we were chatting away amiably as the doors closed.

Then a very large, hairy, freckled hand mysteriously appeared and stopped the lift door from closing. It was Mike with his football kit on his back and he gave us both cheery thumbs up. The next thing that happened was that Mike was followed by ten other members of the office football team and all their heavy football kit bags.

Mr Singh and I glanced at each other as the doors closed but it seemed as though everything was fine. Then the team's eternal substitute Dennis flung first his bag and then himself through the closing doors. Dennis is a very big man and as he landed in the lift, the doors closed and then we set off with abandon.

A second elapsed and suddenly like a shot out of cannon we dropped down fifteen floors at a terrifying juddering speed.

Then with an abrupt jolt we stopped then seeming to defy gravity we flew back up to the top at an even faster pace, shuddering and shaking as we went.

The football team had obviously overloaded the lift and it had developed a very speedy mind of its own.

That morning I saw a whole group of large, grown men cry their eyes out. One after another they set each other off. Somebody at the back shouted "Oh! Please excuse me; I have terrible wind when I am upset."

I do not know how it happened because I had started at the back of the lift but somehow I was now at the front pressing the help button.

"Are you stuck?" said the hoity girl on the switch board.

I answered her with a strange, high pitched, strangled voice that I had never heard before.

"I would love to be stuck, love, but I am going up and down sixteen floors with increasing speed and with much wiggling from side to side with a dozen large, wailing footballers".

I took a deep breath.

"Get the bloody fire brigade….please." I said stiffly.

"There is really no need for that sort of talk" she said, rather too haughtily I thought.

I really cannot tell you how long it went on for but it felt like a very long time. Eventually the fire brigade managed to stop the lift and opened the doors between floors. I was one of the first out and I was secretly glad that I had been on a diet as it was an extremely tight fit.

People came rushing to see if I was alright and somebody called me a taxi and I left the office to go back home. It was about three days later that I remembered the forty people waiting for me to come back with the rest of their course.

For all I know they are still sitting waiting on the twelfth floor of a multi storey building in London.

One evening during the next week I went to do a pre-retirement talk at the BBC. These talks were always fun as everyone was feeling a little demob happy. There must have been two hundred people in the room from the newest recruit to the retiring executives. About half way through we stopped for coffee and the waitress was a little free with the cocoa powder on the cappuccinos.

As everybody settled back in their seat I could feel them all looking at me strangely. I peered out at the assembled crowd and realised every single one had a big chocolate moustache planted firmly on their face. I bent down to get my bag and secretly looked at myself. Sure enough I had a rather fetching chocolate moustache. I took out a tissue and began to rub it off.

A rather elegant woman with perfectly modulated tones in the front row remarked "Thank goodness you have done that we did not know how to tell you!"

I looked out at them and said "Could you all look to the left please and tell your neighbour if you see anything amiss"

It took about twenty minutes for order to be restored as everyone looked so funny.

CHAPTER 56
How nice to see you

Forgiveness is the fragrance that the violet sheds, on the heel that has crushed it.

Mark Twain

Grant cancelled our first appointment but arrived on the doorstep with just thirty minutes notice about three weeks later. As I answered the door I could just about see his head above the biggest bunch of flowers I had ever seen.

There were the deepest of blue hydrangea mop heads interspersed with creamy long stemmed roses and eucalyptus leaves. He had parked his sports car on the drive and looked the part in his linen jacket and jeans. I had given myself a good talking to in the mirror in the downstairs cloakroom as I applied my makeup. The platitudes mounted up in the confined lavender scented space.

I gave myself a sharp, draconian lecture as I stared at my reflection, "You are in your early forties; and even if you say so yourself, you look alright, you have a great job, you are well paid and your youngest child is due to go to University after he has been travelling."

"You have done the hard work now relax and enjoy your life".

"When you think about it, what is left to do? Your broken heart is beginning to mend"….

"The world is full of people and you meet a lot of them in your daily life, it is time to move on"

I had already decided that I would not have Grant back under any circumstances. He was reckless, unreliable and I knew he did not really love me as I loved him.

The fact must be accepted, there was no choice.

Thinking about how I had come to be so disregarded by my husband made me stop in my tracks and made me think long and hard.

I had always believed that there is a perfect, personal synergy of confidence, self-esteem and humility that gives us the ability to follow our dreams and then carve out the most elegant path through our life.

If I applied the pattern to myself then my fault in all these difficulties had been to lack enough personal esteem to expect and then demand better treatment.

A woman friend who is very close to me exclaimed "You just set the bar so low in all the things that you expect from him".

Hurt and with the air knocked out of my chest I said under my breath, "Gosh and here was I thinking I was just honouring my marriage vows."

Then the day came that he did arrive, I opened the door and I supported my shaking body against the door jamb as I took the flowers from him. This was not going to be as easy as I thought.

"Do you want a cup of tea?" I asked. I did not finish the rest of the question as I was in his arms and I knew I could not resist. To my eternal chagrin I think I actually swooned. A little corner of my feminist brain knew I was behaving as malleably as a heroine in a Mills and Boone novel but my feelings for him had always overpowered me.

He was back in my life again and against all odds I thought it was going to be alright this time. That summer was endless and exciting as I was so happy to be with him.

James took his A level exams and our older children came home from University and started spending more time with their Dad. He sold the sports car and bought a red Audi Quatro car that we could all squeeze in at a pinch.

We spent our days taking our beloved Golden Retriever Bella on long country walks and the weeks passed by in a breath-taking mix of pleasure and uncertainty.

I was very busy working long hours and Grant told me he was involved in some new venture. However I was too uncertain and scared of whatever this relationship was turning out to be a mirage to ask anything of him and he offered nothing in return.

The day of the A level results came by and six tall, anxious young men were lying on the front lawn. They were going to school at nine am to collect their results. The postman came and I realised there was a letter from James' chosen university.

I signalled him into the house and ashen faced he ran into the kitchen.

He tore the letter open but all was well, as he had his place for the following year but he kept quiet as all the other boys were anxious.

We celebrated his results and then suddenly we were rushing to get him a work permit and packing his case to leave for Canada and America for a year.

It was only as I was sitting on his huge case to try and close it that I realised he was taking too much baggage. We both laughed at the ridiculousness of what we were doing as he was going to family in both countries and could buy what he needed over there.

We stood at the airport and watched him lope away with his brown leather bag slung over his shoulder and I concentrated on holding back the tears. He was my baby but he was also a grown man of just eighteen going on an amazing journey he would remember all his life.

Father was staying with us and we went up to town to see a show and we saw Carousel which was a disaster as he remembered he had seen with Mother and so I spent the show holding his hand as I knew he was feeling so sad.

CHAPTER 57
Father's big birthday

You have to change your ID. You are not seventy; you are a forty year old with thirty years of experience.

Anonymous

People are usually divided into two camps, there are those who would love a surprise birthday party and there are those who would have the vapours at the very thought of the idea.

Father was going to be seventy soon and we decided that we would throw him a large party as he loved lots of attention and would enjoy the surprise.

My brother Harry and his wife Linda were to be the main party planners as Harry knew most of father's friends and colleagues from The Union and the Labour Party.

Father was with us in Surrey and my main part in the proceedings was to get him to his surprise party on time. He knew something was going to happen and he knew it was going to be held in the North, as we had stayed the night before in a Lakeland hotel.

Father was dressed in his trademark navy suit and red tie and was looking forward to an evening of celebration. We followed the written instructions we had been given and as we drove through ever narrower country lanes he went quieter and paler.

Eventually we pulled up outside a country village hall that had frankly seen better days. We sat in the car staring out into drizzle and gloom. Not one of us said a word, lost in our own thoughts.

Father issued a huge sigh and said "Have the brownies got the night off?" I did not have an answer for him so I kept quiet and calm.

Grant opened the car door and then got out. Father turned to look at me as I was in the back seat,

"How could you let this happen to me?" he complained.

The conversation was interrupted at that point as Grant held open my car door.

"Let's not judge a book by its cover." This was my parting remark to my parent as I straightened both my dress and my face in one fell swoop.

As he entered the front door one hundred and twenty of father's family, friends and former colleagues cheered, waved and clapped.

They were all there that evening, from his Members of Parliament and Trade Union friends to his smallest grandchild, from his oldest boy-hood friend from his early years to his newest lady friends from the bridge club.

Everyone ran towards him and his grandchildren were all so excited and so pleased to see him. I noticed a broad smile on his face.

There were long tables loaded with delicious food and presents and the DJ was playing a combination of father's favourites Nat King Cole , Perry Come and Louis Armstrong singing " *We have all the time in the world*" as well as lots of modern music.

Everybody got up and danced to D:Ream singing " *Things can only get Better,"* *"Them Girls, Them Girls"* by Zig Zag, *"Crocodile Shoes"* by Jimmy Naill *and " Girls just want to have Fun" by* Cyndi Lauper.

There was even a song that involved everybody sitting on the floor as though they were in a rowing boat......

I looked across at Father several times to check that he was engaging with all his guests and he appeared to be having a lot of fun. In my heart I felt a little sad and I wished not for the last time that Mother was still around to share things with him.

I also thought that it was a really wonderful thing to have so many friends and family at this stage of one's life. When we got back to the hotel and chatted over a nightcap he agreed he had spent a wonderful time.

The evening seemed to have given him a new lease of life and he had lots of renewed open invitations to go and visit his friends and family.

The following week Grant and I took him to Lanzarote for a week as his birthday present from us.

If I had known then about the term "Bucket List" then Lanzarote would have been at the bottom of mine but Dad wanted to go and it was his birthday.

We visited bubbling volcanos, sunbathed on black sandy beaches and ate the local delicacy of the smallest potatoes I had ever seen.

The weather was glorious for the whole week. We laughed a lot and enjoyed some lovely restaurants. Flambéed bananas and ice-cream seemed to figure a lot at most meals.

Of course we had a lovely time and on the way home on the plane I gave myself the sage instructions I had given Father outside the Brownie hut ."Let's not judge a book by its cover."

CHAPTER 58
Time for a change in my life

Luck is a very thin wire between survival and disaster, and not many people can keep their balance on it.

Hunter S. Thompson

I had been trying so hard to keep everything going but I was feeling increasingly more tired and more and more of my body felt numb. Relapsing and remitting Multiple Sclerosis has lots of different symptoms and I had had experienced them all at some time or other.

There was an elderly flower seller near my office and one spring morning the enchanting sight of a bucket full of anemones just entranced me. I saw the pink, purple cream and blue faces looking up towards the sun and I could not walk past them. In the language of flowers Anemones are a symbol of anticipation.

I bought four sensational bunches and noticed their hairy stems were tied with raffia. I exchanged pleasantries with the diminutive flower seller and picked up the exquisite bouquet.

I stood waiting to cross the busy road and the last thing I remember was the chilly water from the flowers dripping on to my blouse and then the cold and shocking sensation that made me gasp when the water reached my tummy.

The next thing I remember were unknown faces peering down at me. Of course it was the same old story. I had attempted to cross the road and my legs had buckled underneath me and then I had bumped my head as I fell.

An ambulance had been called and very soon I was on my way to the Atkinson Morley hospital in Wimbledon. I was in for a few days filled with tests and scans, then after a few days allowed home with a warning to take things more easily.

I had decided in my twenties that I would try not to give in to this MS entity but it meant that my existence was filled with episodes of frenetic activity and times of sitting about trying not to feel sorry for myself.

At this time our house was still filled with noise and fun as the children were still in glorious phase of leaving and coming back again. Just when you think there are gone forever they pop back again for a week, a month or a year bringing friends and partners with them.

I have thought about the empty nest syndrome but I am not really sure it exists in the same format anymore. Women who got married in the nineteen sixties and nineteen seventies tended to have a baby quickly after the wedding as despite the hype, free love had not really entered the suburbs and the rural towns.

These young mothers of the nineteen seventies treated their children like precious jewels for whom nothing was too much trouble.

Seventies mother's whole lives were dedicated to making sure these little people had every opportunity.

Fast forward a few years and these seventies women in early middle age had become mothers to well-travelled, highly educated and frankly somewhat spoiled adults.

In common with her generation born in the 1900s my forty-five year old grandmother had a young child of five when I was born. My brother was eight when my first son was born making my mother born in the 1920s a young grandmother.

However there had been a big change in society since then and in most people's families now the children in the family are all grown up when the first grandchild appears.

Mothers who had spent a life-time making their own bread, growing their own vegetables and then rushing to the office were not going to give up their maternal role without a struggle.

In common with many mothers I loved it when I was still the centre of their world and they came back home in between travelling, working abroad and saving up for a house.

Our home wherever we were was always full of people coming and going and I loved that feeling the life was just one long party but I found the daily grind of looking after so many people quite tiring, if I was honest.

I knew that my life was just a natural unfolding of reality. However I really wished I had the emotional and physical energy to make my life my own and not just a reflection of other people's wishes.

CHAPTER 59
A historical snooze

After bad weather comes fine weather.
Maltese proverb

Communication between my husband and me was at an all-time low and I hoped a change would do us good and so I went ahead and booked a holiday in Malta for Grant and myself.

I have always been fascinated by religious history and in fact much to my mother's chagrin the only top grade O level I got was in Religious Education.

I was looking forward to an afternoon at the Valletta History Centre. We walked a long way with our guide and then it appeared that we made our way into a huge cave under the ocean.

We sat on hard, lumpy chairs and waited for the sound track to start along with the film show. The last thing I thought was that the experience was like being at grammar school on a wet Wednesday afternoon.

I am reliably informed that I snored loudly all the way through the thirty minute production and so I knew nothing at all about the Knights Templars, St Paul and Maltese history.

The weather was good that week and I enjoyed the stay but I did not think I would go back again. One day we went by ferry to the tiny, rural Isle of Gozo, which is a smaller version of Malta.

We went to see the remarkable geological stone arch called the Azure Window. Formed millions of years age from a collapsed cave it was worth a visit on its own.

There were elderly, wrinkled and tanned Gozitan ladies outside unfinished houses and they were knitting cream Fair Isle jumpers.

I started chatting to one of these kindly, wise inhabitants and eventually I bought four sweaters from her, one each for the girls and one for me.

When we got home the pale cream jumpers were greeted with much hysteria, which included a ridiculous itching and scratching pantomime as the girls tried to pull them over their perfectly coiffured heads.

Try as I might I could not see the funny side of it especially as I had been forced to leave behind two expensive, precious bottles of fragrant Marsala wine, because of the woolly expanse that filled my case.

The more stony faced I became the more they all screamed with laughter especially when I gave the boys the key rings I had purchased for them.

"Cheeky Beggars" I thought "I am not buying any more presents back from holiday until somebody gives me a grandchild"

In the days after we came back from holiday in Malta we talked about our lives and decided that we really needed to go out a bit more in the evenings. The next few months saw us attending anything and everything we were invited to no matter what it was.

Exhibitions, concerts, dinner parties and galleries were all on our list. However I was beginning to realise that there was still a cavernous expanse between Grant and myself. I tried with all my might to fill it, but only with things of very little consequence that did not involve us getting into deep conversation.

CHAPTER 60
This is a good year for us all

Only those that want everything done for them are bored.
Billy Graham

One morning over breakfast in the sunny garden of the rented house I was still living in, Grant decided to tell me a little about what he had been doing in the previous couple of years. His business was still to do with oil and transport but he said that he was feeling very bored.

That dreaded word again, he was bored...

I did what I always did when he talked about being bored; I tried to see how many words would rhyme with it. This gave me something to think about whilst he talked and appeared to give my face the correct interested countenance.

"Bored, Snored, Maud, Cored, Doored".......

I really was not sure if "doored" was a word but guessed it would do as an explanation if you stubbed your toe very hard in the middle of the night.

Then I was certainly "floored" by his next sentence.

He said that he had thought about it and he had decided if we wanted to be a family it was time to buy a new family home together.

Actually, in reality I had worked long and diligently to get the family finances in order again and to be honest I was nervous of getting involved with him that way again.

However, again I was no match for his reasoning powers, and very soon we began to look for a house to suit us. We found an elegant nineteen sixties square shaped house with leaded windows which had received very little care over the previous decades. It was in need of lots of work but the price reflected that and we both had the skills as we had renovated lots of houses in the past.

We moved into our new home the day before James came back from travelling in North America and Canada.

We were at Heathrow in plenty of time but as luck would have it he was last out of the arrivals gate.

I was actually so anxious by that time that he came round the corner to find his embarrassing mother being told off by the security guard for trying to climb over the barrier to get to him.

Fortunately he loved the new house and was happy because we had chosen a home near to where his best friend Jack lived. However James was going off to University in the autumn and so I was just enjoying having him around for the summer.

Miranda and her boyfriend Alistair graduated that summer and two weeks after we moved we had a marquee in the garden for her and her thirty fellow student friends who had graduated with them. We met all their parents including Alistair's father, Roger, who had been widowed just months before.

Alistair's mother had by all accounts been an intelligent, beautiful and accomplished woman and I knew they all felt the loss keenly.

Just months before Miranda and her cousin Clare had been out to Vancouver to visit James. On the night before our daughter went abroad she had a date with a fellow student she hardly knew but really liked. When she came back from Canada he rang and asked her to go to his mother's funeral with him.

The strange fact is that although my daughter never met her mother-in-law she did in fact go to her funeral. Grant and I attended the memorial service and we were very pleased to have been invited as we met all her friends and family.

Miranda had spent the most amazing time at university and how she and her fellow party goers managed to graduate I will never know.

No matter what time of the day or night it was when you pulled up outside the Georgian house in London that eight of them shared you could hear laughter floating down the street. Not to mention the myriad wine bottles on the step that you had to carefully navigate as a prat fall awaited the unwary. Those very same friends are scattered all around the world now but are still very close. Her best friend Zara is in Australia now but they speak most weeks.

After university Miranda and her boyfriend decided to go travelling for a year and so lived with us whilst they worked for four months before they left on their life affirming trip.

Theo had graduated and spent the summer working as a surveyor before setting off in the autumn to a French University to do an MBA. He had got engaged the previous Christmas to Suzanne and politeness dictated that he ask her rather self-important but generally likeable GP father for her hand in marriage.

Her mother and father were divorced but her father insisted that the announcement could only be formally made in *The Times* the following summer on her twenty first birthday. By that time she would actually have been wearing the perfect three stone diamond ring for six months!

I heard all this with an air of disbelief and wondered if her father knew what century he was living in. There was a lovely engagement party in her Grandmother's garden and I never got a chance to ask Gerald, her father that question, as he seemed to be having such a good time dancing and singing the Beatles karaoke version of *"When I'm Sixty Five."*

CHAPTER 61
We are alone at last

Trip over love, you can get up: fall in love and you fall forever.
Anonymous

Our daughter Miranda and her boyfriend Alistair left for New Zealand, James went off to Manchester University and Theo went to live in Paris.

We heaved a sigh of relief that they were all fulfilling their dreams. I began to think I had done my job and could start to concentrate on my marriage and my career.

Grant and I had never lived alone as Theo was born a year after our wedding. My Canadian Aunt Jane and Uncle Jack had lived with us during that first year as they had sold their delightful English hotel and could not decide whether to go back to Vancouver.

There had been a serious relapse of my Multiple Sclerosis in the autumn and I decided after much thought to make this the time when I gave up the security of my sixteen year Civil Service career.

I loved being with my friends and colleagues and of course having a secure income was great but wanted to branch out into the coaching and therapy career I had been trained for. I loved the thought of working my own hours and the freedom that entailed.

I discussed it with Grant and at the end of what had been a very successful year for the family I finally left my job with not a few tears of regret. The end of my career was going to leave a big hole in my life.

It was very difficult to begin with as I tried to rush out of bed each morning to begin the journey to my office but slowly realisation dawned on me and I had started to claim a few more welcome minutes in bed.

Eventually, slowly I started to enjoy the fact that I could live life at a more relaxed pace.

Now I was no longer tied to office hours I began to see more of my sister Gillian. She had married her childhood sweetheart whilst she was still at University in Manchester.

There is a picture of her smiling in her cap and gown four years later with Mother in her fur coat and hat and Father in his suit with his trademark red tie.

Gillian looked blooming at her graduation ceremony, as she should have been because she was eight months pregnant.

She had been married the first time with all the pomp and ceremony that a first wedding entailed. Mother had designed and then made for her the most fabulous dress with fashionable long sleeves that reached to the floor. With her waist length dark hair she was a picture of radiance and modernity.

Twenty years later we were getting ready for her second wedding. The decision to get married had been a sudden one and so we did not have much time to prepare. The ceremony was three hundred miles north of where we now lived, but undaunted I had ploughed on with preparations. I baked a white chocolate wedding cake and prepared two delicious main courses for twenty guests and borrowed my restaurant owning friends' cool boxes, crockery and flatware for the reception.

There was a choice of beef bourguignon or chicken chasseur for the main course and the much vaunted strawberry millefeuille or chocolate mousse for desert. The day of the wedding the whole lot were now hurtling its merry way up the M6 to the Lake District to the sound of The Fugues new album.

CHAPTER 62
It always rains in the Lake District

Marriage is the triumph of imagination over intelligence; second marriage is the triumph of hope over experience.

Samuel Johnson

As I drove into the glorious Lakeland town that I had spent so many happy years living in I swung by the florists that was owned by my dear friend Doris. We had worked together years before and still kept in touch.

She handed me overflowing armfuls of the stunning amaryllis flowers that I had ordered in both red and white and wished us well. I had asked her to supply me with anything but pink as I knew my sister was wearing red.

My little car screeched to a halt outside my sister's house. I set out the table for the party for later on and put everything in the fridge then checked to make sure Grant had remembered the wine.

I put the cake in the fridge and popped across to the village shop to buy some balloons and when I got back to the house my nephew Rufus had arrived back home. I gave him a hug as I looked out of the rainy window overlooking the hills; I thought how much I adored him.

Two seconds later I opened the fridge and a slice of the wedding cake had disappeared.

"Rufus love, what have you done?," I said quietly. He peered over my shoulder and said "Oh sorry, I did not realise it was an important cake. It is rather delicious!" He and I spent the next ten minutes laughing and artfully rearranging the silk flowers to cover the gap.

As I sorted and organised the fresh flowers I took a deep breath. I was trying to devise a perfect bouquet for the bride and her daughter.

For the bride, red amaryllis with their stems cut short and tied with raffia, with sprays of orange ranunculi tucked here and there and startling white amaryllis with orange gerbera for Claire, her daughter and only bridesmaid.

I hastily made twelve boutonnieres with the scented cream roses I had purchased. I preferred roses as there was something about the ubiquitous carnation that I found sterile and flat even though in flower lore they mean love.

I had made lots of boutonnieres in my time but was just glad that my late mother was not around to see how hurried this attempt was. She hated my occasional slap dash way of doing things. Her sage advice to me had always been, "Slow down, you will yourself coming back, my girl!"

I had already done my makeup but I could not help weeping copiously when I thought of our darling, deceased mother so I had to go back up to the bathroom to apply my best wedding face once again.

Eventually with the flowers in the car and my hat firmly set on my head I set off for the hotel that my sister was getting married from. Grant had gone to Manchester to collect James from University and taken one of his own suits for him to wear as he was about an inch taller than his dad at five foot eleven.

We all arrived at the registry office and my beautiful sister looked divine in her red suit and 1940s style hat. I handed out the damp, windblown flowers as it was another Rainy Lake District day.

We exchanged greetings with the guests and about two minutes after the celebrant started I heard what could only be described as strangled laughter coming from behind me. I looked over to where my brother Harry, his oldest son and my youngest son were sitting and they appeared to be just this side of hysterical with laughter.

When I saw what they were laughing at I had to smile. In the few short months James had been at University he had grown four inches, to match his brother in height exactly. His father's blue suit that he borrowed occasionally was now four inches too short and the turn ups were now just below his very hairy knees.

His rugby player's large calves were on show for the entire world to see. I put my finger to my lips and gave them a stern hush signal and soon the lovely ceremony was over and we all clapped delightedly.

We repaired back to my sister's house for the wedding breakfast. Everyone said that they really enjoyed the celebration food and the formal speeches began pleasantly enough.

I looked out through the picture window at the drizzly Lakeland fells and thought how my sister's divorce ten years earlier had concerned my mother. She would have loved to have known that her youngest daughter was getting married again.

As I was staring at my sister's new husband I noticed that the maroon, velvet dining room curtains had come away from the pelmet at one point and I hoped it would not show up on the photographs. I looked out at the rain soaked fells and thought about how many happy times we had had walking across them in our bright blue cagoules, as an extended family group.

My gaze travelled back to the new husband and he had the temerity to wink at me.

"Cheeky beggar" I thought to myself.

When his turn came to speak he put his arm round my sister's shoulders

"I have always loved Gillian, ever since the day I met her" he began with a smile.

I thought how much like her previous husband he looked except he was a little heavier than him and his hair was definitely a lot greyer.

I took a deep breath and then hurriedly decided to disregard convention and a deep breath gave me the courage to interrupt the groom's speech

"….and if you do not show my sister how much you love this time you will definitely have me to answer to."

My face was smiling but my cool, measured tone of voice meant every word.

He was of course the man who had been my brother-in-law for many years and who my sister had divorced ten years previously.

We all raised a glass to the success of this happy union over the first one and a wonderful day ensued.

That starry night the newly married couple set off for two weeks in the sunny Caribbean, their daughter Claire went back to University and their son Rufus came back to London in the car with us as he was going to the National Youth Theatre for the whole summer.

CHAPTER 63
The Summer season

Note on door, out to lunch: If not back by five out to dinner also.
Anonymous

We have wonderful friends that we originally met through the oil industry. We loved their sparkling company and always had great fun with them.

John, broad and confident with a deep gravelly voice and Jackie, sensible, articulate and glamorous had a really amazing life and were no strangers to the Summer Season.

The Social Season was a throwback of the Eighteenth and Nineteen centuries when it was attended by the landowning and aristocratic families including Members of Parliament but it fell into decline during the First World War 1914-1918.

The modern Summer Season runs between April and August and includes Glyndebourne; this is an English Country House and has been the site of the Glyndebourne Festival Opera since 1934.

The wonderful music of the Proms runs throughout the season and ends at the Royal Albert Hall in early September. The last time we had been to the Royal Albert Hall was to see the peerless Tony Bennett. His voice was still so strong and pure especially when he sung unaccompanied. We had always loved his music but that was the first opportunity we had to see him sing live and we were not disappointed.

The Royal Academy Summer Exhibition for the Arts is an important event. The first Royal Academy of contemporary artists opened on 25th April 1769 and ran until 27th May of the same year.

The exhibition containing 136 works of art were shown and the exhibition known as The Royal Academy Summer exhibition has run annually without interruption to the present day and it is housed in Burlington House, Piccadilly, London

In May the picturesque delight that is the Chelsea flower show fulfils the horticultural aspect of the summer. We attended this show a couple of times but found the number of people with huge back packs there, extremely off putting to say the least. As we were keen gardeners, we were both miles away in our own world, walking hand in hand and enjoying the whole experience.

Our problems only started when a middle aged man, who shall be named Horace, stopped suddenly in front of us. He turned without notice to explain the finer points of a dark purple dahlia to his long suffering wife Mildred. In the process as she turned to take a look, the huge back packs dangling on their backs were flung sideways and actually managed to knock at least four unsuspecting souls to their knees.

They continued on their journey oblivious to the mayhem they had caused, leaving the rest of us to pick the poor people up from the hard, dusty floor. I would have loved to have known the contents of their enormous back pack, guided missiles.

I took an educated guess that it was Tupperware boxes filled with egg sandwiches which sent out a faint effluvia of sulphur and several bottles of warm orange squash, the drinking of which gave you a scratchy throat.

This happened to us a few times and so we gave Chelsea up as a bad job and started going to Hampton Court flower show instead. We took our visitors from other countries to see this delightful floriferous event occasionally and they all adored their historical day out.

We visited on the final day of the show one particular year and subsequently came home with the car full of unusual plants and ferns at knock down prices.

CHAPTER 64
Horse racing and all that

Horse sense is the thing that a horse has which keeps it from betting on people.

W.C. Fields

The horse racing courses to be seen were at Ascot, Badminton, Windsor, Epsom and glorious Good wood on the South Downs.

We managed to go to Ascot every year on Ladies Day and also to The Oaks at Epsom in Surrey. The latter course was only a ten minute drive from our old home in Surrey.

I used to take that week off work as a holiday as you could neither get out of your drive nor back in again as the roads were so busy. My favourite racecourse, if anyone ever asked, was Newmarket and I have really no idea why except for the fact that it feels much less formal than the others.

The spectacular trooping of the Colour was followed by the sporting events. These included The Boat Race, Henley Royal Regatta, Polo, and Wimbledon for the Tennis,

Cowes for the sailing and then of course the Test Match for the quintessentially English cricket matches.

John and Jackie had always been very hospitable to us and we went to the races every year with them. We had also been to Glyndebourne and Henley with them as well as Ascot which I really enjoyed.

Each year we accompanied them to Ladies Day in the Royal Enclosure and as it usually coincided with my birthday I really enjoyed the event. I loved choosing an outfit each year and being up to date with the colours.

It was Queen Anne in 1707 that first recognised that East Cote or latterly Ascot was a great place for the horses to gallop. The Sport of Kings is followed by our own Monarch, Queen Elizabeth the second and there is always a frisson of excitement in the air when she arrives.

The Queen and Prince Philip attend every afternoon of the four day meeting. The Queen and her guests leave Windsor castle at 1.35

pm and drive the short journey in cars to Ascot Gate. There they transfer to horse drawn carriages for the stately procession to the Royal Box.

The expectant crowds get a perfect view of monarch in her plethora of beautiful hats. The Queen first attended in 1945 and has attended every year since then.

The meetings that we know today started with the Gold Cup in 1807 and Ladies Day remains the most popular day of all.

It was very important to be seen and the sight of older but sprightly celebrities with their perfectly turned out wives made the day memorable. A private box was a perfect way to enjoy the day. From canapés and champagne to a four course lunch the food was sublime.

The end of Ascot finds the crowd singing "Land of Hope and Glory" and then the gentlemen flung their perfectly serviceable grey top hats in the air to land with a bump.

This made me smile as the ladies protected their millinery with great care. In fact one particular day when we were there I had spied a neighbour in the crowd and made my way to say hello to her.

As I arrived back in the box the assembled company had left their champagne to stare out over the balcony. Two unknown ladies who were really old enough to know better and whose champagne had gone to their heads, decided to pursue an argument. My conjecture to the group was that it may have started because they appeared to be wearing the same outfit.

Dressed in that year's requisite black and white stripes they looked, for the entire world, like two maniac Andy Pandy puppets with their legs still kicking, as they were pulled apart by two beefy stewards.

What made me laugh was that in all the commotion and rage was that they both had remembered to take off their expensive hats and put them on a nearby drinks table before beginning to shout expletive deletives at each other.

CHAPTER 65
Our lovely weekend away

Politeness is a way of making your guests feels at home: even if you wish they really were.

Anonymous

Our friends John and Jackie had two beautiful daughters that we got to know well. We were invited one weekend to their lovely home overlooking the water front. The house was carved out of a pale mellow stone and had large landscaped gardens. These were immaculately kept by a team of gardeners it took two hours to walk the perimeter.

The welcome we received was unsurpassable and we felt relaxed and happy as their excellent cook made supper for us.

As a first course we had duck consommé followed by lobster tails. These dishes were followed by fillet of beef and spring vegetables and to finish an exquisite chocolate pudding.

The elegant Georgian style house had a full size swimming pool in the basement and eight sumptuous bedrooms. We were allocated a bedroom when we first arrived and a housekeeper took our bags up to our room for us.

When we finally went up to our sleeping accommodation it was to be faced by décor that was absolutely amazing. With shiny blue walls and a king size bed that was an approximation of a Cadillac we could not believe what we were seeing.

The en suite bathroom was equally sparkly and I stood for at least ten minutes just absorbing the decor after I got out of the shower.

After a perfectly lovely evening we lay in bed holding hands trying to go to sleep and then I got the giggles at the incongruity of this jazzy Las Vegas style room in such a glorious, palatial house and after a while Grant tried to shut me up by kissing me.

In fact the harder he kissed me the more I giggled and in the end he just turned his back on me. I tried hard to keep quiet as I did not want our hosts to think we were up to no good and eventually I fell into a kaleidoscope dream-filled sleep. I still treasure the fun we had with them. We eventually moved away and the friendship faded to Christmas cards as so many friendships must.

Life becomes busier and people become more distracted by daily chores and the many responsibilities we all have and only the wonderful memories remain.

CHAPTER 66
Who is ringing that bell?

Learn to say no to the rest: so you can say yes to the best.
John C Maxwell

In the golden late September days of that year the doorbell rang and Bella, our golden retriever barked loudly. Standing there at the front door, pale and wan was my son's fiancée, Suzanne and her over powering mother Glenda.

I liked my future daughter-in-law very much but was not sure what to make of her mother. She was an Anglican vicar and spoke with a soft, smiling voice that rose to an occasional crescendo when she was giving a sermon.

Occasionally you can meet people with a beguiling gentle and soft voiced demeanour that belies their actual purpose. It seems that if someone nods in agreement whilst you are talking and has a kindly voice they can get away with offering their acerbic opinion on just about anything and everything in the whole Universe.

By the time you have absorbed the meaning of exactly what they have said, they are on to their next opinion which they will give you whether you like it or not. This was the case with Glenda, my son's future mother –in-law.

Theo's fiancée Suzanne was in her last year at University but whatever the long convoluted story they were telling me entailed, the upshot was that Glenda wanted her daughter to move in with Grant and I until our son had finished his MBA education in France.

Everything in me that day wanted to shout "Please No" but I listened politely and heard myself say "OK" and she moved in a day later. She was still living with us when they got married a year later.

Just before Christmas my brother Harry who had been working in Germany rang from London. He had been divorced the year before and was missing his three children desperately. He wondered if he could come and stay with us for a while.

The next year saw me with a house full of people looking after my brother's three children at weekends and finding the money to send Suzanne over to Paris as she was missing Theo so much.

My brother lived with us for a few months and then was offered a great job in the North where he could be nearer his children. I was happy to see him go as he was getting on with his life but missed him terribly as he had always been one of the people closest to my heart.

Not long afterwards Harry met a vivacious young woman and they had a short-lived marriage that resulted in a wonderful young man called Rupert. He is clever, funny and kind and as handsome as his Dad and we all adore him.

Not long afterwards my father called on his way to the airport as he was going on holiday with our Canadian family. He stayed overnight and in the morning said over breakfast "I think I am going to come and live with you as I am too young for a pipe and slippers."

Grant and I exchanged glances and then I heard Grant say "Ok sounds like a plan but you must keep your house in the Lakes in case it does not work out."

After we had taken Father to the airport I felt fit to burst, "We really need to think about this as he is only just seventy. He has a life in the same village in the Lakes as my sister, whatever is she going to think about all this?"

"We have plenty of time to decide, but I really think he should keep his house in the Lakes." were my husband's last words on the subject.

I actually thought he was very kind to have replied to his father-in-law that way, I just felt that I needed to think about what it would mean for my life. We decided to talk to Father about it when he came back from his extended trip.

Of course when he came back he had already been in touch with the local estate agents from his holiday home in Canada and he had actually found a buyer for his house in the Lakes.

Two months later his furniture arrived on the drive before he came back from holiday. I absolutely loved my father and he could be great fun but he was actually extremely bossy and totally intransigent.

He was a trade union leader of the old school, he would not brook disagreement at any price.

As I looked out of the window at the furniture van I felt my freedom shrink into a tiny black dot that slowly disappeared off the screen.

CHAPTER 67
The summer of the party

The ornaments of your house will be the guests who frequent it.
Portuguese Proverb

The summer of my youngest son's twenty first birthday was played out against the background of the Olympics in Atlanta, Georgia in America. We enjoyed the Olympics, particularly the athletics and were great fans of Michael Johnson, the 200 and 400 metre champion.

We had always had a summer garden party that coincided with James' birthday.

His birth date was right in the middle of the summer holidays and he had celebrated his birthdays on trains, planes and automobiles.

Just like his older sister Miranda he had kept every friend he had ever made and so his twenty first birthday party attracted a large gathering. We had over a hundred guests in a marquee in the garden including all the neighbours.

Wherever we had lived we had always invited the neighbours as we always enjoyed their company. That and the fact that if they were at the party they were less likely to complain about the noise!

It seemed to me that all our neighbours in this Home Counties Avenue had lived in the same houses since they had been built thirty years before. Their children had all gone to school together and they spent holidays and high days in each other's company. They were all lovely to us and embraced us, as the newcomers, in their circle.

In the months after we moved I had plenty of time to think and it occurred to me that this was the epitome of stockbroker belt. However far you walked, in any direction, which ever front door you knocked on you would find that an accountant, a company director, a solicitor or an engineer would answer the door. A faint reminder of seventies décor pervaded each house.

Orange and brown flowered wallpaper adorned many walls and teak furniture was a requirement in everybody's dining room. In this place, on the whole the men worked and the women played golf or did a little charity work.

I loved the time I lived there but on the whole thought the diversity of city or even village life provided a more exciting way of living.

Politeness dictates that arrangements have to be made in the suburbs. The spontaneity that provides a frisson of excitement in life is lost in the grey mist of whatever is regarded as appropriate there.

The suburbs are perfect when you have children and the family home is a hive of activity. You absolutely need the proximity of schools and a safe and peaceful environment where you know all your neighbours.

However the suburbs can be suffocating for those who are childless or those whose children have finally flown the nest and who feel they have years of exciting things still left to accomplish.

Our wonderful neighbours joined us for James' birthday party that evening and we had great fun from the oldest resident to the youngest cousin.

We had a DJ in the marquee and he seemed to enjoy playing "*Firestarter*" by the Prodigy, "*Macarena*" by Los Del Rio and The Beautiful South's song "*Rotterdam*" more than any others.

This party like all the others before and since went on until dawn. I got up the next morning and stepping over the sleeping young people I thought how proud I was of the twenty somethings they had all become.

One of the benefits my children had accrued from our moving house was that they all had developed the necessary skill of making friends easily.

However it was their kindness and warm personalities that meant once they had made a friend they kept them forever.

I experienced a warm glow of motherly satisfaction as I went to make bacon, eggs and coffee for thirty people.

CHAPTER 68
The centre of the crowd

Behind every cloud is another cloud.
Judy Garland

My father Murray was great fun and loved to be the centre of a crowd but he was still very demanding. Like a lot of women of my age who had been very subservient to their parents I found the habit hard to shake and when he needed something I just complied without question.

My life had turned into an episode of the Walton's with different extended family members coming in and out of all hours and shouting good night to each other. Grant was not really speaking to me and just looked frightfully bored and disgruntled in equal measure.

Grant had not really worked since we moved into the new house but quickly found lots to do when Father came to stay. He was cool and distant with me and whenever I tried to speak to him he waved me away with a flick of his hand.

I knew he really blamed me for the disruption in his life but to be honest I was so exhausted the only words that came into my mind were Grandmother Hester's Sand Fairy Anne (*sans faire rien.*)

For years as a child I wondered what a fairy that lived on the beach had to do with anything. I think I was in my thirties when it dawned on me.

Father had settled in but in the few months since he had been with us he had done so many impetuous things. He had sawn the back door in half so he could lean on it, dug up the beautiful blue conifers in the front garden and then taken the washing machine to the tip because it made a clanking noise.

My poor mouth was set in a constant circular Ooh! shape like the character Olive Oil from the Popeye series.

In fact every time I left the house I did not know what traumatic event I would come back to find. One day he left every single door and window open before he went out for the day. A neighbour rang me to tell me the dogs were out in the road and I came rushing home.

Father answered the telephone for everybody and he engaged whoever was on in the other end of the line in a long, protracted conversation. He gave away our private information to anyone who would listen as if it was so much confetti in the wind and he invented whatever he could not remember or did not know.

Food was a big issue every day and I tried to be obliging by cooking a three course meal every single evening. One day Father said he fancied some liver, onions and cabbage. I made liver and bacon casserole with creamy mashed potato for the two of us as Grant was out that evening. A second after he took the first mouthful he slid his plate under the table for his dog to eat whilst staring at me eyeball to eyeball. I could not decide what I found more disconcerting, his comment on my cooking or the feeding of his poor effluvial hound the cabbage!

As he got up from the table I put my head in my hands and remained there for a while listening to *The News Quiz* on Radio Four. I loved the combination of the sparkling wit of Linda Smith, Alan Coren and Barry Took. Half an hour went by and with a sigh I got up from the table to fill the dishwasher and water the plants.

However, I really did not know how much more of this I could take.

CHAPTER 69
I do not like the ambience in here

In a restaurant choose a table near a waiter.
Jewish Proverb

Father was better behaved whenever Grant was around but that was not very often I am afraid. We would take him to a restaurant and after he had ordered his food he would decide he did not like the ambiance and go and sit in the car before the meal arrived. Those were definitely my indigestion years and a packet of Rennies was always in my handbag.

One particular day my late mother's sister Aunt Beth rang to give me a good telling off because I was not feeding Father proper meals, as he had told her all he had to eat were yoghurts and apples! Whilst she was on the phone she also told me off for making him do all the housework and jobs around the house.

It was really pointless to remark he had not ever lifted a housework finger around the house as I had really stopped defending myself as it felt demeaning and pointless.

Father did make me roar with laugher sometimes and we had fun but other times were just too problematic to deal with. Practical jokes were his specialty and these engendered both humour and a frisson of anxiety deep within my soul. I never quite knew where I was with anything.

There is a theory posited that men start to resemble their mothers as they get older and sometimes it was like living in an episode of the Grandmother Alexandra and Mother-in-law Laura show.

I tried everything to occupy his mind. All my lovely friends included him in their plans. They invited him to dinner parties and concerts and just about anything but it was to no avail.

He was prone to both rhetoric and rudeness in equal measure, I must say he was very fair; he was just absolutely the same with everybody.

My siblings were a great source of comfort when I needed to vent. My aunts all asked if I thought Father was a little "confused" but I knew his mind was as sharp as a tack and it actually still is in his nineties! My smile was fixed but my body was yelling "Slowdown".

I felt so trapped by my ill health and my circumstances that when a family friend asked if I would work one afternoon a week in her children's clothes boutique I jumped at the chance.

I was glad I did as I loved those few hours in that shop as it provided a refuge for my whirling mind and painful body. The perfect designer children's clothes, the tiny cashmere cardigans, the tinkling door bell and the doting grannies for which no expense was spared made for much contentment.

There was one particular grandmother Mrs Ellis, who came in every week and never spent less than two hundred or three hundred pounds a time on her five small grandchildren. She always stayed for a long time chatting to me and I assumed she must be quite lonely as I knew she was a widow.

One afternoon I called in for a cup of tea at a nearby garden centre attached to a local castle. Imagine my surprise when Mrs Ellis served me my tea and a slice of lemon sponge cake she explained that she worked there four days a week and just loved to go shopping on her day off.

There was also another much haughtier grandmother who accompanied her daughter and small children whenever she came in the shop. Her pinched and bowed daughter, who had once been a successful business woman, had been wonderfully successful with IVF at the age of forty two. A year later as luck would have it; the second round of IVF produced twins. The proud processor of three sons under eighteen months of age she had fallen pregnant with a little girl completely naturally. In all my life I have never seen a woman more in need of sleep!

I also met three of my very closest friends in those few months.

Lynne, witty and wise who when she was widowed picked herself up again and began to enjoy a fulfilled life.

Anne, who had everything and then lost it when her husband left suddenly one day had fought to keep her dignity and beautiful home then learned to laugh again on our fun weekend trips.

Jessie, who went back to working in television when her marriage failed and she had a small child to raise,

I loved these strong, powerful women whose lives had not turned out how they thought but with dignity and courage had fought back against adversity.

CHAPTER 70
Lynne

Friends will pick you up when you fall and if they can't they will lie down with you.

Anonymous

My friend Lynne, who had been widowed young and found love again with an old friend, lived in a beautiful country house and worked next door to the Baby Boutique in the elegant Ladies Fashion shop on the village High Street.

Occasionally you meet someone in life with whom you have complete synergy and for me Lynne was one of those people. We had something to talk about wherever and whenever we met. We had things in common, we both came from the same part of the world and had the same number of children but it was a true friendship that arrived from the stratosphere.

She was petite and fashion conscious and every single day was a celebration in Lynne's company.

Every time we went out was an occasion and we would enjoy every minute. Grant, in one of his bored phases, had suggested buying a Winnebago and I asked Lynn to come with me to look at what I would be signing up for.

We looked around every dealership in Surrey and Sussex and got giddier with every visit. A delicious lunch at my favourite restaurant in Brighton completed a wonderful day.

Lynne always had the right tickets for whatever event was on in London. The best restaurants, the newest films and the classical music events of the year were all within her purview. I counted myself very fortunate to be included in her plans when we visited antique fairs, fashion shows and art galleries.

We went each week to the Pilates class that was run by a friend of my daughter. Holly had been a ballet dancer before she had a child and although pleasant, was very strict and there was no option but to concentrate on your core muscles when in her charge. In fact squeezing your core muscles became second nature and you would suddenly find yourself getting a funny look in the greengrocers as you squeezed in time to some imaginary tune.

We also went to water aerobics and that was a completely different matter. Trying to concentrate on the slender, serious instructor left most of us in hysterics. Although I must say that my strength in my legs did improve with all that walking under water.

A winter's afternoon chatting in the kitchen would be made special by a glass of almond flavour Amaretto liqueur wine and some Italian biscotti straight from the oven.

A warm afternoon in the summer house in her immaculate garden would be improved by sherry and a tapas spread of olives, anchovies and chorizo.

A visit to see a concert at the delightful Wallace Collection in Manchester Square, London was great fun. Being able to see the famous Laughing Cavalier painting by Frans Hals from 1664 was a real treat. The four of us girls were in such a good mood when we left the Hungarian Orchestra recital that we decided to throw caution to the wind and jumped in a taxi all the way home to Surrey.

The best thing about my relationship with her though was that she was not afraid to say what she thought. Her insightful remark, "Do you think that by running around looking after everybody else means you do not need to look after your own problems?" made me stop in my tracks.

I felt quite hurt at the time but on examination of the facts decided she was probably quite correct. Sometimes the things with a ring of truth are the ones you do not want to hear.

CHAPTER 71
Anne

Best friends are the ones who are there whenever, wherever, whenever and most importantly forever.

Anonymous

The first time I met Anne I wondered whether she was my kind of woman. She had come to help at the baby boutique to give her an interest in life. Wealthy and recently divorced she was finding life lonely as her youngest son had just gone up to Cambridge.

Elegant but a little old fashioned she was the kind of woman who would never, ever be seen in jeans. A perm and knee length skirts completed the picture. We met twice in those first few weeks and politely and properly circled each other in the proper Home Counties fashion.

The next time I saw her I realised she had been crying and for the first time I could see behind the mask. As we talked I reached out and put my hand on hers and I saw the look of anguish in her eyes.

She had a health problem that turned out to be minor but the support we were able to give each other made us very close.

The mother of three successful sons she had never, ever got over her husband leaving her and it coloured her thinking every day of her life.

Her stories of living in the Middle East when her children were small, were spine tingling and I began to realise that she was courageous as well perfectly mannered.

Kind and generous she opened her beautiful home complete with grand piano to our family from the four corners of the earth who were visiting us for our daughter's wedding. We had such fun together both, when she lived round the corner from me in the Surrey lanes and later when she moved to a picturesque Somerset village.

A visit to her new house in the country was highly anticipated. She had decorated it with the lightest touch and it was elegant and dignified as anticipated. We all sat around in the kitchen whilst she prepared our supper of Sole Veronique. As we sipped our delicious cocktails her hands flew across the fish slicing and rolling the fillets ready to cook at a moment's notice. The green grapes that are the intrinsic part of the dish had to be dunked in boiling water then carefully skinned and pitted after cutting in half. The resultant bounty was put into the fridge to rest.

We repaired to the dining room to enjoy our salmon starter. The candles were reflected in the large antique mirror that she had brought from her previous home.

The main course arrived under a silver dome and we were all a little subdued as the potatoes and broccoli were passed around the mahogany table. We raised our glasses in a toast and began to enjoy the fragrant dish.

Suddenly a piercing scream rent the air and Anne shouted "Stop eating, I have forgotten the grapes!"

She came flying back into the dining room with a dish of freezing grapes and rushing round the table flinging a quarter of the offending green orbs at each plate. For a moment we were stunned into silence and then we all broke into raucous laughter which was still going on at ten pm as we picked our way across the village green towards the local hostelry on that dark, moonless night.

I count the day I met her and the others as serendipitous.

CHAPTER 72
Jessica

Best Friends. It's not a label, it's a promise.
Anonymous

With her dark brown hair and sparkling manner Jessica appeared to be much younger than she really was.

She was part owner of the baby boutique that brought us all together. She had absolutely no idea why she got involved in retail as she had worked in television since she left university.

The only thing she could think was that when she did it she had just had her first and only child in her forties and everything around her had a rosy glow.

She would come in the tiny shop the afternoon I worked there and we would put the world to rights as we served the customers and straightened the racks of divine baby and toddler clothes.

We had perfect small clothes by Absorba, Catamini, Petit Bateau, Ralph Lauren Kids, Oilily, Kickers and many other brands. The most perfect of outfits where every single thing matched. Our best customers were doting grandmothers whose spending power knew no limits.

The co-owner of the boutique was another friend in the village. Gill was a complex mix of warmth and imperiousness. She was always too busy to socialize with the four of us. A successful, handsome husband, who adored her, gave her an imagined elevated position over everything that women with difficult marriages could never hope to possess. She was an excellent artist who had a perfect ability to choose the clothes for the boutique but her haughty manner often confused the people around her.

Jessica had bought a picturesque gabled white house in an acre of tree-lined grounds as the new home for her and her family.

A whirlwind romance with a charming and gregarious man that also worked in television was followed by a wedding in a castle in the highlands.

The four of us women who would probably never have crossed paths became firm friends and had wonderful weekends away where we had such fun. It did not matter where we were either in the most expensive hotel or just round at each other's houses I just loved being with them all.

We would start our trips into London to the theatre or to the symphony very properly and by the end of the evening of sharing stories we would be unable to breathe because we had laughed so much.

Eventually Jessica left her husband as the marriage did not work out and she moved back to Scotland to work in television, Anne sold her beautiful house and moved to Somerset to be nearer her elderly mother and I moved to live in Spain.

Only Lynne stayed in the neighbourhood but we still enjoy catching up from time to time. I learned a lot about life and love from these wonderful women and will always be grateful for their friendship and support.

CHAPTER 73
Up town girl

When the boss is away, work becomes a holiday.

Portuguese proverb

After that early, difficult period settling in with Father living with us, my Aunt Amy's husband John came from Canada to stay with us every single summer.

It made sense having him around as it refocused my father's attention away from me and gave me some freedom. However having a reputation as an excellent cook meant I spent copious hours and amounts of money feeding whoever was in the house at the time.

Murray, my trade union leader father who was seventy and John, my engineer uncle who was nearly sixty at the time often behaved like principal guests at a never ending exclusive cocktail party.

It seemed their pearls of wisdom must be listened to at all costs, if I was not to appear rude. I stood for hours listening to them whilst reciting Jenny Joseph's wonderful poem in my head.

"When I am old I shall wear purple with a red hat that does not go, and doesn't suit me and I shall spend my pension on brandy…"

I recited it in my mind whilst biting my lip, whether that was to stop me laughing or crying I never knew. I recited it on long drives, at the allotment or in bookshops whilst Father pontificated on and on about the length and breadth of his knowledge.

One showery but sunny Sunday morning Grant was out playing golf and I was peeling vegetables in the kitchen. I had been out and picked the last of the beans and realised with pleasure that the leeks, even though they were as slender as daffodil stems, were perfect to eat. We were twelve for lunch that day and before I started the summer pudding I made a pot of coffee and took two cups through to the conservatory.

Sitting in there enjoying the sunshine were my father, my uncle and the dogs. They acknowledged my presence with gracious smiles and went back behind their broadsheets.

Ever since Grant and I had been married we had always taken both the *Observer* and the *Sunday Times*. We had both these delivered on a Sunday morning and today these broadsheets with their many supplements were spread out over the glass conservatory table top.

After putting their cups of coffee down, I begin to glance through the papers on the table. I knew I wanted the Money Section of the *Times*, as I liked to read the back page and also the Observer magazine. Then I smiled at the sleeping dogs as I picked up both sections and looked out with pleasure at my perfect cream and purple fuchsia hanging baskets swaying ever so lightly in the breeze.

As I stepped away, I heard a crisp, business like voice remark "Oh no, no, no!" I stopped in my tracks and looked back towards my father and waited calmly with my eyebrows raised.

He made a little throat clearing sound.

"You must only take one piece of the paper at a time and when you have fully read it you can come back and change it for another one." he said authoritatively.

He shook his paper and looked back down and he did not see me fling the magazine down and walk away on the brink of strangling him.

I should have said "Actually these are my newspapers, as I pay the bloody paper bill in this house and while we are at it, it's my chintz sofa you have your ample bottom resting on" ...but I didn't.

I went into the kitchen and cut a large piece of newly baked carrot cake and took a bite of delicious vanilla frosting. I felt the sweetness slide seductively down my throat and I could not decide whether to laugh or cry.

Instead of doing either I put the radio on very loudly and started to dance around the kitchen, as I always did when any kind of minor difficulty arose.

The music of the moment was Billy Joel's *Uptown Girl* and it served to change my mood from down to back to up again in a few moments.

As I smiled to myself as I thought about a remark I had heard recently.

"Laughter is the best medicine……. but if you don't know why you are laughing ……then you probably need the medicine". Anon.

CHAPTER 74
The VAT inspector

You can dance anywhere even if it is only in your heart
Anonymous

That weekend I also had as house guests two beautiful young ballroom dancers and they wanted some ham and tomato sandwiches for their journey on the train back to Leeds.

I have a cousin on my father's side, Vanessa, who was somewhere in age between my sister Gillian and myself. As a child she had been given to pinching the fleshiest part of your under arm just when you were least expecting it. Just as a yell was forming in your throat you would catch her ferocious stare and think better of mentioning it.

With her red corkscrew ringlets she reminded me of Violet Elizabeth Bott from the Just William series as she always threatened to scream and scream until she was sick if you ever told on her.

This cute little girl had grown up to be a VAT inspector who also enjoyed serving as a Magistrate. In her twenties she had married a kind, older chap and had gone on to give birth to three delightful children.

Their daughter's wedding was a lovely occasion and the arrival of the bride and her father in a horse and cart, in the warm spring sunshine, made the occasion memorable.

We arrived at the wedding a little late and I was carrying two large hats. One was for me and one was for my sister Gillian as her own hats were in storage. She was waiting for me, a little impatiently with her husband Malcolm in the churchyard.

I held out hats, a fancy navy one and a plainer cream one, in front of me. The cream hat was a favourite that I had worn a few times and the navy one was an impulse buy in the sales in Harrogate that I had never tried on. I really hoped Gillian would pick the navy one with its large brim and stunning floral arrangement.

Her hand drifted through the air as she took the cream hat from my grasp and placed it elegantly on her head.

I had to press my lips together to stop a "Noooo!" escaping from them. As she trotted away on four inch heels I plonked the navy confection on my head and followed her a little less elegantly and to be honest somewhat truculently.

We only just made it down the aisle before the bride appeared. Hot and bothered I was squashed in that ancient coastal church's hard pew between my husband Grant and my brother-in-law Malcolm.

I have known Malcolm since we were teenagers in the same year at Grammar school and he has always had the ability to make me become hysterical with his wit and dead pan expression. Slowly as we sat waiting for the service to begin the large, navy floriferous encumbrance began to slide down my head and began to cover my face completely. Everything suddenly went dark but I could have coped, I really could, except for the fact that a deep, gravelly voice next to me offered "Is there anybody there?" in my ear…

Cousin Vanessa's husband Bill still held the family record for the shortest father of the bride speech ever.

He rose to his feet as eighty guests turned their expectant faces towards him. There was a small silence as he coughed and did a little shuffle. Looking towards his increasingly alarmed wife he emitted a strangled "I thank you one and all" and sat down again.

This beat the previous holder of the record, Grants brother-in-law Dennis. A large and experienced detective inspector he stood up and managed "Thank you for coming here today and I..." before bursting into tears.

His wife, my elegant and very proper sister-in-law, took off her spotted, pink silk Condici hat before laying her perfectly made up forehead on the table in front of her, narrowly missing a strawberry iced parfait complete with pouring cream

Cousin Vanessa handsome, youngest boy Rory had become a talented ballroom dancer in his teens and his partner Leanne was an American girl who had come across to England.to dance.

The famous dance school that they attended was about thirty minutes from my house. Each weekend saw them arrive early on Saturday, have a shower and get ready into their dancing clothes and rush out leaving their possessions scattered all over the house. Like any other teenagers they would be back at eight pm starving and collapse in front of the television before staying up late and travelling back to Leeds the next day.

I love people, especially young ones and usually enjoyed their energy but I was really becoming too ill and exhausted to have open house for everyone, all day every day.

CHAPTER 75
The Gothic house

In nothing do men more clearly approach the gods than in giving health to men.

Cicero

One of the reasons for my exhaustion and general crankiness was the fact that I really needed surgery. Like many women I had become increasingly more debilitated by the myriad symptoms that Mother Nature bestows on the unwilling recipients of that hurtle towards the next phase of life, that we laughingly call the menopause. As if this thing that can last many years, was only one particular thing at one particular time.

As you stand on the sloping banks of perimenopause, gently feeling the heat, you can see across to a place of freedom and joy, where you can wear white trousers with insouciance and sport a jaunty hat every single day if you desire.

The postmenopausal state is a spectacular life bonus that leaves you free to live your life as you choose, with the added bonus of a liberated sex life.

However before you get to the other side there is a world of comical symptoms to get through. The fascinating thing is that no two women have the same journey through to the other side.

For me it was standing up in front of a group of people to give a talk that I had given a hundred times before. Then noticing a pigeon flying past the window and following its progress across the London skyline. On returning my gaze to the expectant group I was not able to remember one single word of what I was there to say.

Then periods that became so debilitating that lying on the floor became the only option no matter where you were.

It was this condition that drove me into the arms of a West Country surgeon one April morning.

I knew this new-fangled operation was available with a general anaesthetic in a few hospitals; however the surgeon who had invented the procedure did it whilst you were awake under local anaesthetic. For some unknown reason my stoic self-thought that was a preferable option.

I was advised to stay the night of the surgery within a mile of the hospital in case there were difficulties. Grant came with me and we booked into the bed and breakfast hotel that I had chosen. The proprietor of the large white house welcomed us and said our booking was actually for the house next door where the owners were away on holiday.

She said "Here is the key, we will take your bags over, have a nice stay" in one breathe.

As we walked outside and turned to look up at the gothic monstrosity next door looming above her house she finished with a flourish, "As you will be the only guests there tonight, will you make sure you lock the front door when you go to bed?"

To be honest I was a little anxious about the imminent strangely named microwave procedure so did not really take much notice.

In two minutes we were at the hospital and I was directed to get into a gown and told to lie on a narrow truckle bed. I was soon in the operating theatre and shaking hands politely with the doctor who I had met once before in his elegant consulting rooms.

He introduced three large, young gentlemen colleagues "who are here today to learn about the revolutionary procedure". I smiled politely as I could whilst my legs were being hoisted skywards.

A perfect auburn haired young nurse called Helen was stationed by my left shoulder and she smiled kindly at me.

To begin with there was pleasant cocktail party fare,

"Where do you live? What do you for a living? Where are you going for holidays this year?" and in amongst the chatter an occasional gentle moan escaped from my lips.

After an hour and forty five minutes, I knew the time because I could see the clock, the chatter had stopped and the moaning was no longer gentle. I was feeling just about at the end of my tether when Helen bravely spoke up "I am sorry Doctor but this woman really cannot take any more."

The four male surgeons, dressed in green scrubs, raised their gaze and stared back at me through the gap between my knees. The room was silent for a while and then the chief protagonist boomed in perfect Received Pronunciation,

"Gosh my dear, you must know that women are born to bear genealogical pain!"

Whilst his three serious colleagues nodded their heads in agreement I burst out laughing. I told him that I had never heard such tosh but the surge of endorphins that the laughter had caused rallied my spirits and ten minutes later he declared me well and truly finished.

I thanked him for his expertise and was wheeled back to the ward. As they lifted me back on the bed another nurse came along and said "You have about two hours before we need the bed, I do hope you have somewhere local to stay"

It was actually about six pm when they discharged me. I staggered across the threshold of the gothic style house and as I glanced up I could see the inside décor was immaculate. Grant pushed me up the stairs and got me into bed in the room we had been allocated.

My eyes had been firmly closed and my mind full of dealing with the pain since we left hospital so it was a while before I looked around the room. Leaning over to drink the tea Grant had brought me I realised I was in a large four poster bed in a room that looked like it was part of a film set.

There was not another soul in this dark, stone house. I spent the night kneeling on the floor clutching one of the four mahogany wooden posts moaning softly. Actually the moans could not have been very quiet as at four am Grant said "I cannot take anymore we are going home!"

We crept out into the dark night and he drove gently back to Surrey. The first place I went was to see my doctor to ask for pain relief a little stronger than the ubiquitous paracetamol that they had offered.

Well, I rolled around in agony for about two days but a month later I was feeling brighter than I had felt for a long time.

CHAPTER 76
What about a girls' holiday

If you obey all the rules you miss all the fun.
Lucille Ball

Later that year my friend Lynne asked if I would like to go on holiday with her to Cyprus. It sounded a really perfect idea to my grateful ears as I had been married as a teenager so had never, ever done the girl's holiday thing.

I soon found myself in the long airport queue for Paphos. There were two chaps in front of us and Lynn leaned across and whispered "I don't fancy yours much" which sent me into hysterics. I knew we were going to have a good time.

Lynn is ten years older than me but the most fun of any friend I had ever had. The hotel turned out to be brand new and upwards of five star and so there was everything your heart could desire. There was only one problem; there were hundreds more staff than guests as it had only just opened its doors. The result of this was that every time you went to step through a door there was a handsome young man waiting to open it for you.

Being waited on hand and foot was delightful at first but then it became very amusing and we spent the whole time laughing. Lynn was a very deep sleeper and one night I got up to uses the bathroom and in the darkness crashed heavily into the corner of the wall.

I lay moaning and groaning on the floor Lynn just carried on snoring and sleeping. I gently bashed and banged about as much as I could, desperate for some sympathy but she stayed fast asleep in the arms of Morpheus.

I was a little bit miffed at breakfast that she had not noticed my bruises on display in my off the shoulder t-shirt. We had our usual Greek yoghurt, honey and nuts then decided to go to water aerobics.

I struggled one handed into my fabulous lilac French swimsuit and headed for the pool. A large blue and black bruise that was beginning to form across my shoulder and down my arm matched beautifully with my swimsuit. Lynn and I already went to water aerobics together every week at home and so we knew the drill in the pool.

This was something different again though. The formidable lady instructor shouted the instructions in perfect Greek and the hirsute elderly gentleman beside her, who had a look of Mr Pastry, translated her instructions into English.

This in itself was the source of much mirth. The trouble was every time I tried to swim forward; my damaged shoulder ensured that I went round in a circle.

This happened several times in a row and at one point I went completely under the water. I got the giggles, Lynne got the giggles and they spread like wildfire throughout the class. Eventually the instructor and the translator were laughing so hard that the class had to be abandoned.

We spent the afternoon sunbathing and drinking cocktails with our new friends from aerobics. The Cypriot Filfar orange liqueur is delicious with a splash of white wine and ice in a hot climate. It evokes the taste of oranges, sunshine and the pure white blossom in a crystal glass.

However the bottle of the delicious nectar that I carried carefully home with me did not really taste of much at all.

I wonder why that is always the case?

CHAPTER 77
The French and the Americans

Everything is funny as long as it is happening to somebody else.
Will Rogers

A part of the course of Theo's French MBA degree was to be spent in America. The flights to Boston and Paris were cheaper from Gatwick and so my helpful first born had arranged for six French students to stay with us for a week and a month later six American students stayed with us for a week going the other way.

The reason he gave was that we lived about an hour from Gatwick. We had little notice but managed to sort out beds and catering arrangements before they arrived.

In my experience of having visitors from other countries to stay I had realised something profound. If one or even two people from another country come to stay they tend to blend in. However if three or more land on your doorstep you tend to get a real flavour of the differences in nationalities.

The first students to arrive were five French men and a young woman called Valerie. I use the term students loosely as because it was a post graduate MBA course they were all in their early twenties. We made them welcome, cooked for them and the first evening sat down to have a very pleasant conversation.

Our house had a lovely galleried landing and as I loved photographs I used this elegant and well lit space to display many portraits. There were graduation photos, wedding photos and lots of others from happy times over the years. I have to admit that as a proud mother the graduation photos were a little more prominent than the others.

The next morning when I arose I found the delightful Jean Paul standing half way down the stairs staring at these pictures through his round Harry Potter glasses. We exchanged a smile and he assured me that he had slept well.

We went into the kitchen together and as I poured him a cup of coffee I sensed he had something to say. "Madame, you know in France it would be considered bad manners to display photographs like you have done on your walls. It would be seen as....What would you say...showing off."

I was just lifting my coffee cup to my lips and smiled a much tighter lipped smile at him. "Thank you for that salient information Jean Paul and if I ever go to live in France I shall bear it in mind. However I would like you to remember that in England we consider it bad manners to make disparaging remarks about other people's homes whilst they are in the room," and with that I took my coffee into the garden.

We really enjoyed their visit and Valerie was particularly helpful and friendly. She told me about her family who had a small farm in Brittany. Her mother had never ever worked outside the home and loved her garden. She remarked in perfect English that her mother disagreed with working mothers in principle, as a mother's place is at home with her child.

I smiled but did not respond but wondered just how many days a week she needed to be home for her twenty five year old, only child.

A couple of weeks later the American visitors arrived. All were men this time and keen to discover the sites of London. One of the chaps Brad asked me whether politeness would dictate that he should leave his bedroom door open when he went out as he did at home.

"I do not think we have a rule here on that, whatever suits you," was my reply.

Theo came back from America having had a wonderful time. Our guests all wrote to say thank you and I discovered two things about the Americans, they hated the rich food they were served in France and they kept their bedroom doors open when they were out. I also discovered two things about the French. They hated the low fat meals they had been offered in America and they kept their bedroom doors firmly closed whilst they were out.

However, the best surprise was left for me until last. A week after Theo's wedding, when he was still on honeymoon, there was a knock on the door.

It was Valerie from Brittany standing there with a ruck sack on her shoulder. "Was I expecting her?" she asked politely.

Keeping my smile in place I invited her in.

When she opened her rucksack I noticed that it contained dozens of bottles of Slimfast and two changes of clothes.

It turned out that she had got an internship in London for three months and Theo had of course assured her his mother would not mind if she stayed in our house and travelled up to London each day!

CHAPTER 78
The foundation garment

Curve, the loveliest distance between two points
Mae West

I had missed my daughter so much whilst she had been away. Miranda and Alistair had travelled all around the Far East and then spent six months working in New Zealand. Alistair's late mother was from New Zealand and so they met all his cousins and aunts whilst they were out there working on a kiwi fruit farm.

They decided to come home for Theo's wedding and rang from San Francisco to say they would be home two days before the actual wedding day.

My daughter rang and said "Please, Mum do not make a fuss at the airport like you did with James as I could not bear it."

"Cheers" I thought I have not seen you for a year and I am not even allowed to jump up and down with glee.

We waited excitedly at Heathrow Airport and Grant said, "We will be able to tell by their body language whether the trip was a success on not".

They walked round the corner holding each other's hand tightly and we smiled as we thought they made a perfect couple. As I reached her I accepted her proffered cheek and I remarked, "How lovely it is to see you, darling," when all I wanted to do was jump up and down and hug her to me.

My oldest son Theo spent that year in France and arrived home at the end of July of that year having finished his studies. His wedding had been planned to the last detail without him and all he had to do was turn up three weeks later at the church.

His bride Suzanne, who was still living with us at that time, had become so thin in the weeks before the wedding that I was worried about her and spent my time making tasty meals to keep up her strength. I followed her round with a bottle of Minadex which was full of vitamins and minerals and that made her laugh. She made occasional visits to see Theo and him drove back home to England as often as he could.

Her curly haired, bespectacled GP father met her in town to take her to Harrods to buy her wedding gown but other than that we did not see either of her parents in the time she was with us.

As was my nature I had done all my research for Mother of the Groom etiquette. It seems that the Mother of the Bride always got first choice regarding the colour outfit she would wear on the day. I made several rebuffed enquiries about colour choices and with two months to go I still had no idea what Glenda would be wearing.

I made a shopping trip into Manchester with my sister Gillian and my then eighteen year old niece Claire. After much discussion over lunch we decided cream and navy would not clash with anyone else's colours and we set about our task.

Three hours later I was trying on a fitted Windsmoor cream dress and jacket in the Kendal Milne department store. My niece put her head through the curtain and I noticed a little frown playing about her forehead.

"Mm, it's very nice Aunt but you do realise you will need a decent foundation garment under it, don't you? She opined.

After she closed the curtains I allowed myself a little chuckle.

The last person I had heard mention a foundation garment was Mrs Raymond, the Spirella lady from round the corner in Robins Wood Road the 1960s. She provided the neighbourhood ladies with stiff and unyielding whalebone corsets in shades of white, cream and the palest of pink silk.

I remember the brass plaque outside her house announcing this fact to the world. Of course Mother never, ever had need of her professional services being the proud possessor of a twenty two inch waist for all her life.

"Gosh, that saying must be back in vogue" I thought as I decided to keep the afore mentioned dress and jacket with its delightful matching buttons.

We could not find a suitable hat that day but a solo trip to a well-known milliner provided the solution. This gentleman had hats in every colour and style in his fashionable emporium. He decided that a wide brimmed navy fedora with a cream ribbon would be "just the ticket".

I was not exactly sure about the look, but he firmly reminded me that "I am the expert, you know!"

Well, I think that was what he said, as his voice was muffled by the heavy curtain behind which he had gone to put my card through the machine.

I cursed my size eight feet not for the first time. I searched shoe shops all over town for a perfect place, where all beautiful creations would be made in my size. Eventually I plumped for a pair of very high but sensible navy shoes from Marks and Spencer and I was ready to go to my son's wedding.

CHAPTER 79
Carmen Miranda's hat

I never follow what people say is fashionable A woman must always wear what fits her.

Carmen Miranda

O f course, eventually I found that perfect shoe Shangri-La when I started to go visiting The States on a regular basis. It transpired that this amazing place had shopping malls where every single shoe shop had perfect shoes and best of all in my size.

Every time I returned from the other side of the Atlantic I could be seen carrying bags full of boots, work shoes, dancing shoes and wisps of nothing shoes just because I could get into and then stand up in them.

The only person I mentioned my reservations about the coming nuptials to was my sister as I knew she kept my confidences. I told her I actually thought they should wait a year to marry until my student son had a job and they were both a little older.

On the day before the wedding Grant and I spent a wonderful few hours with our beloved son shopping to buy presents for his best man and ushers. We spent the hours just talking together and walking around Chelsea in the shimmering August heat.

A delicious lunch of seafood salad gave us the opportunity to tell him how proud we were of all his achievements and how much we loved him.

I have attended weddings all over the world and each society has a different rhythm to the countdown days. I love the North American idea of a rehearsal dinner and the elegance of the evening before the big day, dressed in finery and meeting the important guests.

There is no tradition of this in Great Britain but there is something to be said for holding your child close for just one more day.

The wedding day dawned perfectly warm and clear and we all set off for Suffolk. We checked into our hotel and soon it was time to head for the church. I was feeling nervous and even more so when Theo's good friend Sam arrived on a Harley Davidson to take him to his wedding.

His best man was our younger son James and he followed behind on another motorbike. My heart was in my mouth all the way along the dual carriageway and it did not start beating properly again until I saw them both waiting outside the church.

The funniest thing was that as we entered the cavernous, ancient church in which they were married it was to see the bride's mother standing on the left dressed severely from head to toe in sepulchral black.

She had on a long black skirt, flowing black jacket and huge black hat with a veil that covered her eyes.

I laughed when I thought I could have worn a fruity hat like Carmen Miranda and orange kimono with blue spots and still not clashed with her.

Glenda, the monochrome mother of the bride had her own elegant mother standing beside her in the church in an ancient mink coat and hat, even though it was a sizzling August day.

Suzanne's grandmother, Eliza who called everybody "Darling" in the manner of Zsa Zsa Gabor, always looked immaculate, as though she was ready to go shopping in Harrods at a moment's notice.

I thought she was wonderful, if a little right wing in her views but I always enjoyed her charming company.

CHAPTER 80
A perfect day in August

The secret of a happy marriage remains a secret.
Henry Youngman

With a capacity for over a thousand worshipers St Mary's Church is one of the largest and oldest parish churches in the country and is rumoured to have the longest aisle. Nothing remains of the Norman church and the one that stands there in its place was built in 1290. However a splendid Norman Tower is located by the Cathedral.

The church is along the same row of buildings as the Cathedral and is where Mary Tudor, sister of Henry the eighth is buried. Her tomb rests in the Sanctuary directly to the north of the high altar. The gothic architecture is spectacular and the stained glass windows provide a spectacular show on a sunlit evening.

The flowers in the church were wonderful. Scented white lilies and perfect pink peonies decorated every pew. We smiled at all our family and friends as we took our seats at the front pew on the right. I looked at my husband sitting by my side and we exchanged smiles.

My father was seated on my other side and I could see he was holding both his and my mother's wedding rings in his hand and so I reached out to squeeze his free hand.

Miranda, my daughter was doing the reading of Shakespeare sonnet 116, which is universally known as the Paean to Eternal Love. Every family wedding in recent times had included this beautiful, haunting sonnet. The words rang out powerfully around the packed historic church.

> *Let me not to the marriage of true minds.*
> *Admit impediments. Love is not love*
> *Which alters when it alteration finds,*
> *Or bends with the remover to remove;*
> *Oh no! It is an ever fixed mark*
> *That looks on tempests and is never shaken;*

It is the star to every wandering bark,
Whose worth's unknown, although his height be taken,
Loves not times fool, through rosy lips and cheeks
Within his bending sickles compass come:
Love alters not within brief hours and weeks,
But bears it out, even to the edge of doom.
If this be error and upon me proved,
I never writ, nor no man ever loved.

I looked across at my daughter and we exchanged a smile of reassurance. She looked so tanned and beautiful after coming back from her worldwide trip. I glanced up at my two tall, handsome sons and thought how proud of them I was.

Then the first soaring notes of Handel's Arrival of the Queen of Sheba began and I burst into floods of tears as I struggled to my feet.

When Suzanne passed us I thought how beautiful she looked in her strapless shantung silk gown and matching hat. She was a very attractive girl and they made a really handsome couple. Her flowers were exquisite, a cascade of white calla lilies and cymbidium orchids.

I could not stop the tears falling and so I gave into them with little shuddering breaths. When the service was over we repaired to the registry and then the ordeal of the longest and most slippery aisle in England loomed before me.

Hanging on to the arm of an extremely haughty man I hardly knew, whilst tottering along in four inch heels was not an easy task to accomplish. I found smiling and nodding in a very hot hat made the task even more difficult. I was glad when I got out into the sunshine and I could finally let go of his reluctant arm.

I had been advised that he was not very happy as he had been instructed that his beloved, if a little unsuitable fiancé, was not to make an appearance under any circumstances.

I had actually met her at a function and thought she seemed to be a rather charming woman.

The day was very formal and so after we arrived at the stately home where the reception was being held there was champagne and croquet on the lawns as we were waiting for the photographs to be taken.

When I glanced across at the bride and groom I thought how happy they looked together and I thought in my heart that was all that really mattered in the end.

I did not know it then but within a few weeks they would be back living with us again, so they could save up for a house. Actually not much really changed at all that lovely day!

CHAPTER 81
The forsaken Mantilla

Spouse, someone who stands by you through the trouble you would not have had if you had stayed single.

Anonymous

Many years before I had worked in an office in the small town in which we lived. Being young and naive I had not realised that amongst my mainly middle aged, church going colleagues there was an affair of the heart being conducted under a veil of supposed secrecy.

The gentleman involved was called Cedric. He was the executive manager of the office I worked in and he had lots of airs and graces. His favourite saying offered to all and sundry was "Two ears and one mouth, use them appropriately."

It was his answer to everything no matter what the question. He occasionally if pushed would venture "Let's all make sure we are singing from the same hymn sheet," or offer his favourite homily "There is no i in team" and that made me want to scream.

He would shout "Come" in a very precipitous manner when anybody knocked on his door. He was quite short and only his silver head appeared over his mahogany desk when you entered his domain. The effort not to laugh at his pomposity required real self-control.

His delightful wife, Emily, a kind and unassuming woman also worked at the office.

Then there was Ruth, a single woman of uncertain years, who was a keep fit fanatic. She always seemed to be loitering on the stairs when the silver haired Titan named Cedric passed her by. She seemed to drop her files at the moment he appeared and they always seemed to be bent down in a huddle.

Eventually, I was there long enough to be let into the office secret about the dalliance that had been going on for many years.

Ruth, the keep fanatic sat next to a woman called Ethel, a maths genius, and although they were colleagues they certainly were not friends.

Ethel, the maths genius lived in a very nice bungalow with a nice lady called Mildred, a keen needlework aficionado, on the other side of town.

It would have remained like that in perpetuity except for the fact that Emily, the wife, whilst gardening one Sunday afternoon had a massive heart attack and died there and then.

We were all devastated as Emily had been very popular and she had been particularly kind to me when I first started work.

Well, Ruth, the keep fit fanatic just assumed that after a decent period her position in the Titan's affections would be secure. However much to everyone's amazement it did not work out like that at all.

Offices are always places of gossip and innuendo but nobody could have made up the following story.

In a few short months Ruth, the single keep fit fanatic and Mildred, the older needlework aficionado had been relieved of their romantic positions and Ethel, the maths genius and Cedric, the Titan, after a short engagement, were to be found kneeling at the altar in their local Presbyterian church.

Suffice to say there was a bit of a kerfuffle in St Marks that Saturday and although Ethel's elegant shantung silk wedding dress remained unscathed, her rather fetching Spanish mantilla ended up squashed on the floor of the vestry!

CHAPTER 82
The play at the Savoy

For the theatre one needs long arms. An artist with short arms can never make a fine gesture!

Sarah Bernhardt

We all loved the theatre and went as often as we could. This particular trip there were ten of us in the party included my sister Gillian and husband Malcolm who were driving down from the Lake District.

We had tickets to see JB Priestley's *When We Are Married* with Dawn French, Alison Steadman and Leo Mckern which when I bought them I thought would please the women more than the men.

We waited outside the Savoy Theatre in the Strand for all the party to arrive and we made our way in. I knew this area of London well as our daughter Miranda had worked at Coutts Bank for a long time.

This lovely theatre had been sadly ravaged by fire in 1990 but was now beautifully re-created and had been opened in 1993 with a performance by the Royal Ballet.

The original theatre had been built by Rupert D' Oyly Carte. The original opening night in 1929 was a revival of Gilbert and Sullivan's *The Gondoliers*.

I had not told the crowd that the only seats I could get together were in the Upper Circle. In the Savoy Theatre these are very high and considerably further away from the action than the dress circle and the stalls. As the party climbed higher, the moaning increased and there was lots of huffing and puffing as we made it to our seats. My brother-in- law went to get drinks and came back saying "I think I have just been served by an angel". This made everyone around us laugh.

Grant disappeared to the lavatory and I had to stand up to let him get behind me. I whispered, for his ears only, as holding my waist he squeezed gently past me "Oh my goodness sir, I think I have just joined the mile high club."

Of course everyone around us heard as well and hysterical mayhem ensued.

We enjoyed the play and then headed for a Chinese restaurant for a late convivial supper.

CHAPTER 83
The dogs are still asleep

Let sleeping dogs lie.
Robert Walpole

It was very late when we arrived home but I had spent the afternoon making beds up for everybody and I had left the house in a perfect state for visitors. I had remembered everything except a key to the door. In the group of people who were standing around looking at me I could count at least five who actually had a set of keys to the house...... but of course it was my fault.

After a few false starts it was decided that Theo was the appropriate person to climb in the bathroom window. My oldest son is a tall man with broad shoulders but with the agility of a cat and was soon up the drain pipe, across the garage and into the house. It was just about that time that somebody mentioned the fact that the dogs had not barked even though we had been loitering noisily for thirty minutes.

When Theo opened the front door he said "Come and look at this." Two very large dogs were fast asleep in front of the Aga lying on the kitchen floor. They were obviously not a lot of use for guarding the house.

The next night we were going to a friend's birthday party and Theo was driving his Dads new BMW car.

Grant usually listened to Radio Three and so when the engine started a classical piece popped up. Bending down to turn the radio up Theo said "I love Mozart" and in one fell swoop put his foot down and sent the prized automatic car hurtling forwards instead of backwards.

We sat stunned for a moment as we realised he had driven straight into the heavy garage door causing quite a lot of damage.

As steam shot out of the radiator we all burst out laughing and had to repair to the kitchen to get a grip on ourselves before venturing out by taxi.

Of course the next morning it did not seem so amusing but a quick call to a local builder soon had the problem rectified

However our oldest son has never been allowed to listen to Mozart again as it obviously disturbs his molecules.

CHAPTER 84
Home again, home again

The most beautiful view is the one I share with you.
Anonymous

My daughter Miranda and her boyfriend bought a lovely mews house in London, my youngest son James was living in halls of residence accommodation but the newly married couple came back to live with us for a while. Theo had myriad qualifications but he wanted to work in the City so he had to start at the bottom.

Theo and Suzanne lived with us for another year which was fine with me but the house was full of people most of the time. Theo soon excelled and when they did buy a house a year later it was a majestic eight bedroomed Georgian town house which needed a lot of work but it became a labour of love for them.

Once I had decided to start studying again life had more structure but I was hoping against hope for an improvement in my physical condition as I did not seem to be any better.

As well as my family we also had Grant's family with us a lot of the time. His mother was towards eighty but still as sharp as a tack and still issuing instructions to all and sundry.

She still insisted on ironing Grant's shirts as she had always considered that I did an imperfect job and that was fine by me. We also had his youngest sister Faith to stay every holiday as she was a single parent with a difficult teenage son who needed Grant's influence.

All his sisters decided to go on holiday together and asked if we would have Grant's mother for a few weeks. I said what I always said which was "Yes "and we went north to collect her. For a few weeks I had my father, my uncle and Grant's mother staying with us as well as two big dogs. I smiled until my face hurt.

One night I heard such a commotion and alarmed, flew out of bed. It appeared that my mother-in-law, Laura was trying to climb out of the bedroom window. My father, Murray hearing the commotion had run to her bedroom and now had hold of her ankles trying to stop her from falling onto her head in the rockery.

For a millisecond I considered that my life was like a Brian Rix farce and then I ran to help recover her dignity as her nightie was over her head and her ample derriere was available to be viewed by any passer-by on that star filled, warm night.

My father was absolutely wonderful and helped me pull her back inside.

Grant slept through it all and when we finally got his mother back in bed I took one look at her eyes and realised that she had had a stroke. I managed to get her comfortable and then called the ambulance.

My mother-in-law Laura had always been quite glamorous when she was younger and it made me smile to realise that between being taken ill and having an oxygen mask put on her face by the paramedics she had managed to comb her hair and put her lipstick on.

It was whilst waiting by my mother-in-law's hospital bedside when she was sleeping that I began to think about her life.

I gazed at my mother-in-law's calm, sleeping face and thought back to that first day I when I met her when I was just fourteen years old and she was just in her forties.

As a child you think your family is normal until you become part of another one and then you realise that every family is completely different. My mother-in-law Laura was so different to my mother Mona.

Laura had an opinion on everything and she voiced it regularly but Mona would not have told you even if your hair was on fire. Mother-in-law Laura nipped upstairs to clean the four bedrooms with the spray can of Pledge in one hand and a large, yellow duster in the other. To my child like amazement she was back twenty minutes later ready to do something more interesting that involved putting lipstick on and going out of the house to see her sisters.

My mother Mona thought spray polish was the lazy man's way and would spend at least four hours with the proper tin of lavender polish and she remembered to turn the mattress on the bed at least once a week. Mona was in bed by nine rain or shine but always up at six am. Laura would start ironing at two am but getting up was a struggle.

My father Murray paid all the bills and had been as steady as a rock as far as finance was concerned. His whole raisin d'etre was to make sure that his wife was spared the stresses of daily life. He had always opined to my sister and me that "In a successful marriage the man should always love the woman more than the woman loves the man." Of course that was the last thing on our minds, as at fourteen years old we both chose the men we were going to love and spend the rest of our lives with.

It was obvious from the start that we both loved them much more than they loved us but that did not seem to matter to anyone at the time.

My father-in-law however was cut from an entirely different cloth. He was irresponsible, charming and a really hopeless husband and Laura adored him. The first time my mother-in-law ever had any money was when she got a job at a city centre bank as a widow in her fifties. To her amazement she was really good at business and soon got the promotion she deserved and was able to buy herself the finer things in life.

I became lost in the reverie of being a girl again when mother-in-law awakened and the doctor arrived to examine her. I stayed at the hospital with her all day and then got home at seven pm.

I realised then that neither of my housemates had thought about supper and so I stood and made spaghetti bolognaise with a green salad and a cheesecake.

Laura finally came out of hospital to convalesce at our house but it was obvious she was going to need a lot of care going forwards. We had loved having with us but she wanted to go back North where she felt she belonged and eventually she began to recover some of her previous spirit.

She had always been so independent and considered not being able to go to the library on her own or to the cinema with her friends a very severe consequence of infirmity and advancing age.

It occurred to me then that people who have always been home-centred like my mother Mona cope more easily with the consequences of being home bound. People like Laura or my paternal grandmother Alexandra who have used their home as a base from which to travel and have fun in their lives can find the confinement of infirmity stifling.

CHAPTER 85
A chronic insomniac

Who looks outside, dreams: who looks inside awakes
Carl Jung

I had been a chronic insomniac since my 1950s childhood even from before I knew what the words meant. Long before the age of real understanding had arrived I knew who in our home had already entered the hypnagogic state, by the tiny sounds I could hear in the dark.

My father had a deep sonorous breathing style which calmed and reassured me. My mother, who never, ever moved after she had disappeared under the covers for the night, occasionally sighed.

This barely audible emitting sound from her had such a wistful, haunting air that I always very worried to know if she was breathing properly.

I had been known to go in and check Mother sometimes by putting a little mirror under nose to check she was still breathing. I had seen this done in Dixon of Dock Green which was one of the few programmes we were allowed to watch in the early days of television.

I used my favourite doll Hetty's little blue plastic mirror but it was really too small to mist up properly so I just stood very still and stared until I was reassured that she was breathing, then I could go back to bed and resume my honouree position of guardian of the world.

It never occurred to me that if she had woken up and seen my little face peering directly into hers she would probably have had a heart attack anyway.

My little sister Gillian, who I shared a room with until I married, squeaked occasionally when she turned over.

That faded childhood bedroom containing two small beds and a chest of drawers that were fragranced mainly by lavender furniture polish. The was also another underlying scent of yellow Wrights Cold Tar Soap, pink medicinal Euthymol Toothpaste, and green Soft Soap shampoo that had to be made with boiling water.

The resultant green, gloopy liquid was never quite cool enough when it was poured on your poor little head and there was always a shout of "ouch, ouch!"

Copious bottles of the ubiquitous Parazone bleach were stored everywhere in our home along with the faint hint of suffering that was deemed good for your soul.

There was also an underlying scent of geraniums as Mother over wintered her plants in the lavatory, which was next door to the bedroom.

The powerful smell of these plants and the tortuous abrasive Izal loo roll that felt like a cross between greased proof paper and a hedgehog made this solemn, freezing place to run in and out of quick smart.

My early childhood bedroom was at the back of our home, so completely dark with no hint of light anywhere.

However I could transport myself all around the world in my child's vivid imagination. The only problem was my world consisted of our tiny home, the church, my school and the shops we frequented on a daily basis.

There was a field behind our house and behind that the school with its 1950 style flat roof. One Christmas Eve I heard a noise outside and climbing up on to the chest of drawers I was able to see out of the window. I was only five years old as my little sister Gillian was still in her cot in mother and father's room.

When I looked out of the window I saw Father Christmas in his sleigh land on the roof of the school. The sight was mesmerising with the full complement of large reindeers and red and green flashing lights. Father Christmas was in full scarlet regalia had a whip in his hand and as he flashed it the sleigh flew up in the air and disappeared into the night sky.

When I told my mother what I had seen she frowned and said " I don't think so, darling" and I could not convince her. However when

January came around and I was back at school I won a Christmas story completion and I was very pleased.

However I was deflated when I read the remarks that said "Good use of imagination" which meant they had not realised I had really seen Father Christmas either!

However my favourite place to travel to, in in my mind, in those dark empty night hours was my Grandmother Hester's house where, in some ways, everything felt as though it would be alright.

CHAPTER 86
The bed under the window

I am not asleep but that does not mean I am really awake.

Anonymous

I really loved it when my brother Harry was two, my sister Gillian was nine and I was thirteen years old, as we three children all shared the eight foot square bedroom at the front of the tiny flat we called home. Harry and Gillian had bunk beds and I slept under the front window with perfect access to a magical land of sights and sounds that filtered through the pale blue sprigged cotton curtains.

I knew there was a big world out there.

A large, red double decker bus passed every ten minutes and I wondered where those people were going at this time of night. I could hear late night revellers from the many pubs around us and exhausted shift workers chatting as they headed home.

There was a pub on the corner that Father was allowed to go to on a Friday evening for three hours only. Mother thought any more than that calamity and ruin lay along the road, for all of us. Occasionally I heard an expletive outside in the street that I knew existed but would never, ever be heard in our very proper home.

It was the light show that entranced me the most. A certain gap in the curtains left an elongated triangle across the ceiling that constantly moved and morphed as cars came down the road opposite our home, affording me the occasional glimpse of my precious siblings faces.

If I stretched my chilly foot out as far as I could, I reached the safety of the heavy wooden drawers and somehow that calmed and centred me in the lonely, nocturnal journey of my mind.

As a small child I talked to my mother about my inability to sleep. Mother, who always went to bed at nine pm rain or shine including New Year's Eve, had two solutions.

"Close your eyes as your body is getting the rest it needs, but it will get even more rest if you are quiet as a mouse" or more frequently "Say your prayers my dear, then God will hear you and….. *Put you to sleep*".

I did not like the sound of the second solution since I had heard what had happened to Rex the next doors neighbour's Alsatian dog when he was taken ill.

This news flooded me with fear once more and I added this to my list of worries.

Nothing ever worked as I was still awake as the clock chimed midnight and bounding up by five am the next morning ready to be helpful another day.

CHAPTER 87
The hour of the wolf

The best cure for insomnia is lots of sleep.
W.C. Fields

Insomnia was a boon when my children were small especially as my oldest son seemed to have inherited my "shut your eyes at your peril" complex. He was still awake after midnight and up again before the dawn chorus asking complicated questions before he opened his eyes.

In the days before Google that meant many trips to the library.

It was however, so lonely in the small hours of the night before the advent of night time radio and television. I was relaxed until two thirty am as that was yesterday and I was positive after four thirty am as that was tomorrow.

The two hours between two thirty five am and four thirty five am were my difficult hours when the weight of the world pressed on my chest. I did not realise that other people felt the same as me until just after my autumn wedding in 1968.

I hated scary films with a passion and somehow unintentionally read an advert for Ingmar Bergman's surrealist "The Hour of the Wolf" in the *Manchester Evening News*.

It brought another troubled perspective to my thinking.

"The hour of the wolf is the hour between night and dawn. It is the hour when most people die, when sleep is deepest, when nightmares are most real. It is the hour when the sleepless are haunted by their deepest fear, when ghosts and demons are most powerful."

"Bloody Hell," I thought, "I am glad I did not know that when I was a child as it would have finished me off completely."

I used to iron in those sleep deprived hours and one night I stepped into the kitchen to get the little plastic jug that I used to put water in my steam iron.

I noticed the jug sitting there on the dresser already full of water and so I picked it up and lazily poured the liquid into the top of the iron.

My eyes were focused upon the bronze jug of fat, yellow King Alfred daffodils that I had picked in the garden earlier in the day and the powerful scent suddenly assaulted my nose and I sneezed loudly, several times. The first lines of a long forgotten poem from school days drifted through my mind.

"I wandered lonely as a cloud that floats on high o e'r vales and hills, when all at once I saw a crowd, a host of golden daffodils".

Two things crossed my mind at once, William Wordsworth and Thorntons Toffee. I knew what the Wordsworth connection was but I could not for the life of me understand the very strong smell of toffee in the room. I was beginning to think I was developing synaesthesia.

Of course this incident happened in the 1970s when every modern home had a Soda Stream fizzy drink maker. Someone, who shall remain nameless, had left the remnants of the lemonade sugar syrup in my tall, white china ironing jug.

I had in turn had poured the colourless liquid in my new iron and because my head was in the clouds I had started to iron the collar of my husband's brand new white linen shirt with molten toffee. My sleepless night cost me the price of a new iron and an even more expensive shirt the next morning.

CHAPTER 88
The Cinderella hour

The early morning has gold in its mouth.
Benjamin Franklin

The majority of my sleepless nights would go something like this....

The familiar Newsnight music would drift to an end and Peter Snow, John Tusa or later Jeremy Paxman would wish us all a polite good night. Gathering my thoughts I would sit for a little while and contemplate the world and its tricky current political situation.

Then the clock would strike the Cinderella hour and with a sigh I would head up to bed. Laying there for a while and feeling a tickly throat coming on so I would lean over for a drink of water "That will not quench my thirst," I would think, "I know I will go and make a nice cup of tea".

I would sit at the kitchen table with my tea and stare round the room and notice how much I loved that particular kitchen and the quiet in the early hours.

"Should I have a digestive biscuit or a homemade shortbread to go with this tea,?" I would ponder.

This was the eternal night time question that played on my mind. Giving in to temptation meant sharing half of whatever it was with Bella our Golden Retriever and then I would go back to bed five minutes later.

The mahogany tallcase hall clock would tick loudly as I realised that the dreaded dyspeptic discomfort was upon me. After suffering for twenty minutes I would think "I really need an indigestion tablet and they are downstairs in the kitchen drawer". It never occurred to me to put them in the nightstand.

I would wander back into the kitchen and then have to have a long drink of water to wash away the taste of the indigestion tablet and then gingerly climb back into bed so as not to waken my peacefully sleeping husband.

Minutes later I would say to myself, "Oh no, I need the loo now, what with all that tea," so I would tootle off quietly to the en suite bathroom.

By the time I got back in bed the birds were singing and light was dawning. "I may as well read now, it's not worth going back to sleep" and I would nod off for two hours leaning back uncomfortably against squashed pillows. I always had three stacks of books by my bed.

The easy to read books were usually detective stories by Ed McBain, Raymond Chandler or Agatha Christie.

The mid-range books, usually a feminist biography or two including those by Gloria Steinem or Simone De Beauvoir as the history of women's lives fascinated me.

The difficult books were usually the classics. This pile stocked up alarmingly and definitely wonkily and included Willkie Collins, *The Woman in White* and *A Tale of Two* Cities by Charles Dickens.

"It was the best of times, it was the worst of times…" like most of life if you think about it.

I also had my favourites that I read over and over including *On the Road* by Jack Kerouac, *I Know Why the Caged Birds Sing* by Maya Angelou, *Cider with Rosie* by Laurie Lee and anything by Doris Lessing, which were usually scattered on the floor somewhere.

My reading glasses were always balanced precariously on the end of my nose giving me a look of a demented Eric Morecambe.

I could go weeks without proper sleep before I finally gave in to exhaustion and then would sleep right through until the next morning.

PART THREE

CHAPTER 89
She occasionally flaps her wings

Despite my thirty years of research into the woman soul, I have not been able to answer the great question that has never been answered ,"What does a woman want?"

Sigmund Freud.

I was only forty-five years old when my oldest child got married but after the excitement of Theo and Suzanne's wedding had passed I began to wonder what the next steps were for me.

My health was a real problem as another Multiple Sclerosis relapse had appeared and I was now walking slowly and unsteadily with a rather jaunty flowered cane.

I had gone from feeling like a slip of a glamorous young thing to doing a wonky approximation of the Old Queen Mary.

Some days I just could not get out of bed and the mysterious white owl I had named "Misery" occasionally flapped her wings around my empty mind.

I was sitting in bed one morning drinking a cup of tea and eating a rather large croissant. As I licked the delicious homemade raspberry jam from around my lips I happened to look down at my prone form. After careful examination I concluded

"Tomorrow I will definitely go back to plain porridge and a half a banana."

The staccato words echoed around an empty room.

I descended slowly downstairs silently passing my two needy house mates and from my rosewood desk took an ancient Basildon bond pad and my mother's favourite fountain pen. I stood for a moment staring mindlessly through the leaded window at the front garden.

Then I noticed the pink and pale yellow, over-blown, scented roses sitting before me in a small crystal rose bowl that I had owned since my early marriage. There was a small crack in the rim where a helpful soul had put it in the dishwasher, but as it did not influence its efficacy in any way so I thought it was a shame to throw it away.

I lifted the bowl up carefully and inhaled deeply. This simple act caused some of the outer petals to float carelessly back down on to the polished desk in a pleasing pattern.

The smell was divine, but then I remembered my mother's sage warning about a lady she knew who inhaled a greenfly and had to go to hospital.

That easily remembered vignette made me laugh out loud as I put the bowl gently back down.

I climbed back up the staircase slowly and then scrambled back into bed with a little list, both real and metaphorical.

The main heading that I wrote, in the careful italics that I had learned in childhood, on the cream watermarked paper were as follows:

You really have to get a grip my girl.

Next I attended to the subsections in order

The first one was, *"What was wrong?"* and I feared that it might be a long list.

The second subject was, *"What was I capable of doing?"*

The third one was, *"What did I want?"*

I decided to do the third list first as I thought it might be the shortest list.

Just as I was about to put pen to paper again my father came bounding into my bedroom like Tigger in The House at Pooh Corner.

I loved the fact that he had boundless energy and enthusiasm but I was no longer well enough to be a social secretary for his every waking moment.

"What's on today then?" he said rubbing his hands.

"I am not sure Dad, will you give me an hour and would you go and make sure Bella and Billy are all right, please," I asked pleasantly.

My father had brought a very large black and white Heinz fifty seven variety style dog called Billy when he came to live with us. My father Murray and his constantly moulting but largely lovable dog ruled the house.

Father was convinced Billy's main component was sheepdog whereas I was convinced it was a Great Dane. My husband, Grant and my father, Murray had developed a kind of Mexican standoff about whose responsibility it was to clear my lovely garden every day.

In fact I was the only one who could not stand the mess so it was a daily trauma for me and my dignity.

That morning I settled back into bed for the duration.

Looking at the perfect italics my unsettled mind flew back to the childhood Cadbury's handwriting competitions that always took place around Easter time. Fortunately I usually won a prize and with the crisp white certificate came the delicious bounty.

It was always chocolate in its many guises and memories of the delicious taste sent me scurrying to remove a Crunchie out of my dressing table drawer. I looked at the clock and it was eight thirty am but I was sure the sun was over the chocolate yard arm somewhere in the world.

I stared at the blank page and looked around for a book to lean on. The one I found was ironically a copy of *Bleak House* by Charles Dickens that was on my bedside table and it really made me laugh out loud.

I checked the pen would write and after a little jiggling and squiggling I wrote.:-

Number 1. *What do I want?*   Then I underlined it three times.

To begin with I stared mindlessly and then eventually glared ferociously at the shiny cream expanse of Basildon Bond.

My head seemed to be completely empty.

How could I possibly know the answer to the question about what I wanted as I had never asked myself that question in my life before now?

I was still thinking closely about that knotty problem when I discovered that the delicious Crunchie had completely disappeared, as if by magic.

CHAPTER 90
The expensive face cream

Ageing is not a lost youth but a new stage of opportunity and strength.
Betty Friedan

I got up to wash my hands and stared at my familiar face in the mirror. Unbidden, my crackled early morning words appeared from nowhere, "Hmm, are those a few more broken capillaries I spy?... Yes, just the ticket," echoed around the north facing bathroom.

I pulled my face this way and that, always upwards never down, to see if there had been any overnight improvement.

I looked about the bathroom and realised that the regal pot of face cream, my darling daughter had bought me as a treat, was still sitting there.

Cream De Mer announced the label and I gathered it was something to do with the sea. It smelled lovely so I dotted the luxurious cream all over my face and neck. It made my face look much better so I slathered it on my hands as well.

When I told Miranda she laughed, "Oh! Mother, you have used that miracle face cream for hand cream. Have you any idea how much that cost, it was over a hundred pounds, that's why there is a tiny little scoop with it".

"I stand corrected" I answered stiffly "I will be more careful in future".

I struggled along the corridor back from the bedroom and climbed back in bed for the third time that morning. Putting on breakfast television I readdressed the issue of, what do I want?

Staring at the empty page my attention was caught by a segment on the television about ageing and plastic surgery so I concentrated on that instead.

I have often wondered about what I would have done if I won a plastic surgery competition. I guessed it would be to lose my dratted stomach that seemed to have a life of its own. I am afraid it even stuck out when as a slip of a girl I did some modelling for my then employer Marks and Spencer.

We have a black and white photograph of Alexandra my paternal grandmother playing cricket when she was about thirty years old. She bequeathed me her hair, her complexion and her rounded figure.

She walked every day, never worried about anything and drank the water that the vegetables had been boiled in, as she believed in the goodness of vitamins.

After fondly reminiscing about her and her long life for a little while I resumed the thinking position.

Eventually the perfect response to the posed question,

"*What do I want?*" came to me like a bolt of lightning and I wrote it down and underlined twice in red.

"*The truth is I am not sure what I want is available to me.*"

CHAPTER 91
The book collector

Anyone who says they have only one life to live must not know how to read a book.

Anonymous

That particular morning when I finally arose my father told me he wanted to go to the book store in Guilford and then proceed to buy himself a new pair of walking shoes.

Father was an avid collector of books and before he left the family home in the Lake District he had given away several thousand volumes to the Labour Party.

He and my mother had both been voracious readers and sometimes could go hours without speaking because they were so engrossed in whatever historical or political opus they were reading at the time.

Father had begun collecting books again whilst living at my house. The trouble was that having grown up with books I was also a bibliophile and so every wall in the house groaned under the weight of these tomes.

I did not mind being in Waterstones or Hatchards book shops but sometimes wondered why I was wasting my forties standing behind my father whilst he discussed the relative merits of socialism and capitalism with the elderly bibliopole in some dusty emporium.

I came to the conclusion that because most of the time I did not feel well enough to argue the finer points of my case for freedom with anybody: that I should just adjust my cane to support my tingling arms and increasingly more troublesome legs.

In a corner of my mind I knew the constant turmoil in my life was making me feel as though I was on an eighteenth century carousel, in some ancient sea side resort where the wind whistled and the sun rarely shone. It was always a crepuscular time of day when I attempted to climb back up again on one of those faded gilt, smooth wooden horses. Then suddenly the ride would speed up again faster and faster with its constant centrifugal force. Suddenly I would be catapulted off again in a high luminous arc and as I fall to earth the coarse, gritty sand would bite into my knees and hands, leaving me breathless and giddy with shock.

That evening I cooked a delicious meal of pork and mushrooms in Marsala cream sauce. I attempted a desultory conversation but everyone was lost in their own thoughts and another evening went slowly by.

CHAPTER 92
My mother's dressing-making skills

All you need is love but a little chocolate now and then does not hurt.
Charles Shulz

By the time I had filled the dish washer and fed the dogs and watered the plants in the greenhouse it was eight pm in the evening before I finally got two minutes to myself to continue my list making and chocolate eating.

I went back upstairs and sidled back into bed after a busy day and I finally felt able to think more clearly.

"What was I capable of doing in my current state?"

Not sticking up for myself with the people I loved that were for sure. I knew this was my own doing, as intellectually I knew that the only person's behaviour you can change is your own and nobody likes a martyr. However no matter how hard I tried I could not find a pathway towards exerting my own thoughts and wishes.

However I thought this subject of what I was capable of would be a breeze and that I could find lots of things to accomplish.

Except I couldn't write the list because the pen had disappeared After a long search that ended with me realising I was sitting on the royal blue, crystal encrusted, Jaeger Christmas present pen, I started in earnest.

It did however cross my mind that if I ate a few less chocolate bars and croissants I might have noticed where the pen was sooner.

The List.

a) I could become a more accomplished cook.

Well I had done a cordon bleu course years before but in my experience the more people enjoyed your food the more they kept coming back for your highly regarded hospitality.

I loved baking with small children but little people were in short supply in our family at this time. I also loved eating the delicious morsels that I concocted as evidenced by the bouncy castle that I was currently sitting upon.

b) I could be a better gardener. Well I could, but the actual stuff of gardening was physically beyond me at the moment. I decided to spend more time in the greenhouse and was determined to ask Grant to put me a chair and heater in there this weekend.

I had a bright idea and I wrote "Register for a flower arranging course" and reaching round for the utilitarian red pen put a satisfyingly large red tick by this idea.

c) I could do more interior design. Well I could, but painting walls was beyond me at the moment and I was never a capable seamstress much to my mother's chagrin.

My mother had been an exquisite maker of all things beautiful out of the tiniest scraps of delicate material. Cushions, curtains and quilts were her speciality.

She had also made my exquisite wedding dress in which I felt like the most beautiful woman on earth. A long white silk sleeveless column with a neckline that left space for my great grandmother Hannah's cream pearls. Then a guipure lace coat with a long train on which she had sown hundreds of pearl buttons.

She was so talented but everything took so long as she was a perfectionist. My sister and I wore matching clothes every day until I was about twelve years old and Gillian was eight. The neighbourhood children regularly teased us about our pristine appearance but we actually thought we were so lucky to be the most cared for children on the block.

With that long forgotten phenomenon absorbing my puzzled mind, I began to listen to *The Moral Maze* with Michael Berk and thought for a while about the opinions that had been expressed. This programme was one of my favourites but occasionally the opinions made me a little hot under the collar.

It never occurred to me that was the whole point of the programme really until years later.

I allowed my mind to wander and Irene Thomas popped into my head. She had been a regular contestant on *Round Britain quiz*. I loved this programme and thought her and John Julius Norwich had voices that were perfectly pitched for radio. I noticed in her biography that *The Telegraph* had called her omnipresent and I think that perfectly described her charming radio presence.

My mother was rather perturbed when the tune Radioscopies by Georges Deere was replaced by a more modern one on *Round Britain Quiz*

Then mother's face disappeared from my mind as I dragged my recalcitrant brain back to the present day.

Right… I wrote.

I decided there and then that I would have to start using my brain again until my body got back with the programme.

Thoughts about my coaching and therapy skills took over and I decided to enrol myself on yet another useful course when I was feeling better. One thing led to another and the next day I was talking to a wonderful man I knew who lived in the Pyrenees and who gave me great advice for my future career development.

Many years before I had read and reread Agatha Christie's biography. In this she mentions that she had noticed that women of around fifty years of age suddenly develop a huge thirst for knowledge.

Being a great fan of her books, I had on my bookshelf every one of the Miss Marple books in beautiful navy blue leather bindings. I had discovered these in an Oxfam book shop many moons before and I happily paid the twenty five pound price tag for these now treasured possessions.

I decided that Agatha was completely correct and I was going to slake my thirst for knowledge with a vengeance.

I was going to study, write and think until my brain hurt.

CHAPTER 93
The What was wrong list

When anything goes it's the women that lose.
Camellia Puglia

It was ten pm the next night when I climbed back into bed clutching my list in one hand and a cup of tea in the other. I left my husband Grant and my father Murray watching the World Snooker Championships in the den and so I thought I would not be disturbed for a while.

Nothing of note came to my mind and so eventually I got out of bed and slipped out of the back door into my beautiful garden. The last of the lilac night scented stock that looked so plain in the day, came alive at night and filled the air with an exquisite scent.

I sat on the ancient wooden bench and pulled my much loved but ancient cardigan around my chest. I did not need a list to tell me what my problems were.

I took a frayed band out of my pyjama pocket and wound my hair into a pony tail high on top of my head.

I peered right down to the bottom of the garden at my greenhouse of abundance, whose shimmering panes were reflecting the night's Hunters moon.

Then suddenly startled, I came face to face with the ghostly grey elephant that constantly haunted every room in my mind.

I knew in every fibre of my being that there was a seismic fault at the heart of my marriage; I just did not know what it was. I had nursed my husband through several bouts of depression in his life but

I could never really understand what the underlying problem was with him.

Of course I thought the fault was mine. If only I was taller, thinner, sexier, cleverer or simply better at everything, he would suddenly be happy and love me....

I pulled my knees up under my chin and adjusted my position in the chilled night air. As I breathed a deep shuddering, sigh in the diffuse moonlight I made myself a list of promises to be dealt with the following day.

I promised myself that:

No 1. I was going to talk to my father about demanding less of my time and about being more respectful of the woman I had become, not the compliant child I had been. I wondered why I had always found this conversation with him so difficult.

No 2. I was going to see the neurologist and get a proper prognosis for my health and wellbeing. I needed to know what the future held for me as far as my health was concerned so that I could plan properly.

No 3. I was going to talk to Grant about what he really wanted and then I would finally accept it, as a fait accompli, if what he wanted was not me. I was going to tell him if we were going to stay together he had to get a job and start enjoying our life together.

No 4. I was going to embark properly on my coaching career and use all the training that I had worked so hard for.

No 5. I was going to go to Canada the following week to take up an open invitation to stay with the family and have some time out of time.

CHAPTER 94
Bright and early

The truth will set you free, but first of all it will piss you off.
Gloria Steinem

The next morning I was up very early as I had not slept a wink. I found my father in the kitchen at seven am doing the *Times* crossword. He did this everyday as he felt it kept his brain sharp.

After I had made a cup of Earl Grey tea and put some eggs to boil I began my well-rehearsed utterances.

"Please, Dad I need to talk to you" I said quietly. "I love having you here with me but I need a life as well. You are suffocating me. Please find something to do so that you are not so bored when I am out of the house"

He listened to me under his Dennis Healey eyebrows and I could not tell from his green eyed stare whether he agreed or not but he nodded his head when I finished talking. He gave me a hug and I felt much happier. I loved him dearly and wished not for the first time that my mother had lived to share these years with him.

A few days later I saw the new neurologist at Atkinson Morley Hospital. He was very kind and listened quietly to my garbled entreaties. He shrugged his shoulders and said "You are going to have to live the best life you can, until you really can't live it anymore."

The young consultant took a deep breath and then said "If it's any comfort if you are not in a wheelchair now the chances are good that you may not be in one for a long time."

Basically it was the old story of mixing a soupcon of stoicism with a bushel of pain relief and after taking a deep breath just get on with it.

It made me smile to think that when I was first diagnosed the prevalent thinking was that there was absolutely no pain with MS. When you complained about the pain, the specialist, as we called them, advised an area just above your head that it might be "your nerves my dear."

That day I went home and spoke to my Aunt Amy on the telephone and then booked my flight to Vancouver before I spoke to Grant.

Trying to pin him down was always an ordeal so I deliberately took a seat on the piano stool near the double doors that led to the hall.

I loved that stool and I had covered it to match the elegant long cream curtains that dressed every set of windows in the sitting room and I also matched the shades on the crystal lamps and chandeliers.

I could see through into the conservatory and noticed that the goldfish we named Silver and Goldie were back in the sunshine. I burst out laughing as I had always kept the ancient goldfish in the kitchen as it was cooler in there but Father kept moving them back into the sunny, airless conservatory in his eternal game of "Guess who is in charge in this house?"

I realised I had lost my focus and quickly turned my eyes to look at the familiar stranger who was my husband. I explained that I was going away for two weeks as I needed a break.

"I never know where you are and I cannot rely on you and I need more out of our marriage as we get older" I said firmly all in one breathe. "I love you with all my heart," I finished.

"Yes I know you do" was his cool, measured response.

We stared at each other for a long moment and then I said "You need some focus, a new career to capture your interest and you need to earn some money. You should only stay if you want to be with me because we have a long time to live yet".

I said the last sentence to the silver framed photographs on the piano as my husband had already left the room.

When my daughter came to visit me later that day, I said to her, "Miranda, I am at the end of my tether."

She stared at me for a long moment and smiling fondly announced, "Mother, I have never met anybody who had such a long one" and that made us both giggle.

I told my two sons I was having a holiday with the family and the next day I was eating a delicious but solitary cream tea staring out over the vast expanse that is Greenland.

As I flew over the Canadian Artic Archipelago I wondered why this far off place was more associated with Europe, particularly Denmark rather than as a part of North America where it seemed to belong.

CHAPTER 95
Two weeks of fun

Canada is like a bird, it likes to soar freely.
Anonymous

My aunt Amy met me at Vancouver airport with a bunch of yellow freesias, as flowers are the delightful Canadian way. I had never flown alone before but came to the conclusion that you could get lost more easily in a bus station than in an airport.

Amy had been travelling backwards and forwards on her own to England since the early 1960s. The first time I went to meet her at the airport she was dressed in a navy skirt suit and white blouse and wearing high heels. She also had on white gloves, a jaunty navy hat with a small veil and pink lipstick. She looked elegant and poised, if a little hot because she was carrying a tiny baby, a toddler and steadying a four year old who was trying to hide behind her skirt.

Those three little blonde cherubs had been sitting on her knee for over ten hours. They came at the right time on that visit because their Grandmother Hester got to meet them before she passed away.

Her whole family made me so welcome in those two weeks I spent in Canada. I knew them all well of course because they had stayed with us every time they had been in England. Amy was a wonderful letter writer who could paint pictures with words and kept the whole extended family in touch with each other's news. I still have most of her letters.

Amy is only thirteen years older than me but I had always held her in very high regard. My childhood self, believed she had the answer to everything and her constant high spirits were a beacon of light in my life.

Mother was the oldest of the four sisters and Amy was the youngest, but they shared the same features. Except that where my mother was tall and slim her little sister Amy was smaller and daintier.

I was so delighted to see her and although I did not want to bother her with my woes, I did want to bask in the rosy glow that surrounded her.

Although I loved my father dearly he was driving me crazy with his constant demands but I could not mention that here. Father was revered by all my mother's brothers and sisters as most of them had been children when he met his future bride.

Amy's husband John was also Father's travelling companion. They had travelled all over Europe, Canada and America in a large Winnebago. I actually thought Aunt Amy was a saint for not complaining when her husband left to come to England for months on end, or disappeared on an American jaunt with my father.

CHAPTER 96
I love this place

Eat, drink and be scary.
Anonymous

Whilst I was in Canada there was great excitement over Halloween. October has always been my favourite month with reds, yellows and oranges of nature and the faint scent of wood smoke in the air.

However Halloween always made me vaguely anxious and when my children were small any mention of going out dressed as a witch would have been met with a very definite negative response.

The Canadians and North Americans put a lot of effort into decorating their homes. Halloween parties are prevalent and each house has a large box of candy to give to children who knock on the door in fancy dress and shout "trick or treat!"

The ubiquitous orange pumpkin has a dual purpose of becoming either a lantern or a pot of soup and both things can be found in people's homes at the end of October. Every house has its own recipe for toffee apples, roasted corn or pumpkin pie.

This October when I was visiting I spent a special day with each of my cousins.

Joanna had just discovered she was expecting her first baby and I set about knitting baby jackets for some reason. I had not knitted for years but the simple act of repetition and creativity calmed and steadied me.

Joanna and I had a lovely day at the Museum of British Columbia with its first nation artefacts. Then she took me back to her house on the Island for a delicious lunch. Her garden ended where the ocean began and it seemed an idyllic place to bring up a child. Watching her ocean going sail boat bobbing about on the water I thought it seemed to be an idyllic life but knew she had to leave at five am every morning to start her day as an accountant in the City.

Her sister Sienna who was a manager in an insurance company in Vancouver arranged to take her mother and I to the theatre one evening. We had such a lot of fun as Sienna has a great sense of humour and her laugh was very infectious. Blonde and beautiful she turned heads wherever she went.

I met my cousin Joshua down town another day. A partner in a law firm he had lots to do but had perfected the art of always making you feel he had all the time in the world for you. His mother Amy and I enjoyed the Japanese food we were treated to and then had a fun shopping trip where we tried on all the latest fashions.

Amy and I travelled across to Vancouver Island to see my Aunt Jane and her husband Jack. They had lived in England when I was a teenager and I had been close to them.

We had a wonderful few days in their newly built home not far from the beach. The town itself was perfect with every kind of old fashioned store and it reminded me of the place where Jessica Fletcher lived in *Murder She Wrote*.

One day we visited Victoria, the capital city and had a walk round the British Columbian parliament and then took afternoon tea in the Grosvenor Hotel.

The famous hanging baskets that gave this place such an English feel were beginning to fade but never the less provided a spectacular show. I was sad to leave Jane and Jack but said we would see them in England soon as they were planning a trip.

A few days later Amy took me to their holiday cottage up on the Sunshine Coast and whilst we were there she went to singing practice.

She had sung with the Sweet Adelines since she arrived in Canada in the 1950s and had travelled all over the world with her choir.

Virginia, who was the choir mistress, invited us to tea at her house and whist pouring earl grey into her Royal Albert Old Country Roses cups she suddenly said "And what are you dear?"

I had dreaded this question because although I came from a musical family I really could not sing. I loved music but by some misfortune when I opened my mouth all that came out was a croak.

"Soprano, Mezzo, Contralto," and then she caught my giggling aunt shaking her head. "She really cannot sing," she just about managed.

I loved the Sweet Adeline concert I went to see, but thought all that faux smiling must be very hard on the cheeks.

The second week I was in Vancouver, Uncle John and Aunt Amy took me out and about to some wonderful places. It was lovely to be a tourist but I especially enjoyed the time Amy and I had on our own to talk.

We chatted about everything and nothing whilst sipping hot chocolate by the fire as the cold snap had arrived without warning.

Aunt Amy and I were very tearful as we went our separate ways at the airport but soon I was winging my way back to my family and my own life.

The flight was uneventful and nearly empty and gave me time to reflect on the next phase of my life.

CHAPTER 97
Home again, home again

Welcome to our society, you will be judged on what you wear, what you look like, how you act and your taste in music.

Anonymous

I arrived home two weeks later having had a wonderful time. Travelling on my own had given me a sense of freedom and a soaring confidence in my abilities even though I was unsteady on my feet.

My youngest son, James came to meet me with a big bear hug at the airport and explained to me that his Dad had just been offered a new job. He said he was on good form and looking forward to seeing me and sharing his news. I was really pleased about this as I had been dreading coming home to more trouble and strife.

Hours later I was bending down putting a load of whites in the washing machine when I saw a shadow move across the laundry room wall. As I stood up straight Grant was standing behind me with a big smile on his face. He was holding a small bunch of rather insipid looking carnations that looked like he had picked them up at the petrol station two minutes ago.

"Hi love," he said frowning "Are you alright?"

I smiled a tight lipped smile and with one hand behind me to steady myself I leaned gingerly back against the tumble dryer.

"I am fine thank you," I replied.

"Look here, I am just going to say this once" he shrugged "I am really sorry, but I will try much harder in future and I do love you".

And that was it, no discussion, no explanation; he had nothing to say to me except, "I will try harder."

Something had changed inside me whilst I had been away and that night when he put his arms around me I must admit I was a little less enthralled by his charms.

We decided to do a little more in an evening and went to the cinema to see *The English Patient* the next week. I usually love Ralph Fiennes but we both came out feeling sad and a little distracted. We saw *The Birdcage* the following week with Robin Williams and Nathan Lane and that made us both laugh.

We went up to the National Opera to see *The Marriage of Figaro* which we both thoroughly enjoyed and came out determined to go at least once a month. Like all things your intentions are good but somehow fall by the way side because of work and other commitments.

I spent some months on a Life coaching course in Central London. I enjoyed meeting new people from different places and walks of life. Christopher, the Canadian former Tibetan monk who led the course was worldly wise and an excellent teacher and we still keep in touch.

I was in my forties, with a lot of my life's responsibilities discharged but I had the feeling that the most exciting adventures were yet to come, as long as I could keep well.

Grant and I were very polite to each other and I really hoped that we could start to repair our relationship.

We had completely opposing views on a lot of things including our choices in contemporary music.

When I was in the house on my own I played Nina Simone, Savage Garden, Crowded House and Elvis Costello very loudly. I also listened to Radio Four in every room for preference.

Grant listened to Radio Three and preferred Elvis, The Beatles, Frank Sinatra and Johnny Cash to anything else.

Maybe there should be a question about music when the vicar gives you the pre-marriage talk!

CHAPTER 98
A political family

> Hell I never vote for anybody. I always vote against.
> *W.C. Fields*

I had been raised in a very political family. Whilst other families discussed general chit chat around the dinner table we were treated to long diatribes about the state of the country, the economy and the history of the Unions.

If you refused to go on a march for the worker's rights or South Africa you could be persona non grata for a while. A Christmas lunch would usually end with a collection for Oxfam or Save the Children and there was usually a rendition of the paean to socialism, *The Red Flag.*

I knew all the twelve of the verses from "The people's flag is deepest red...to we'll keep the red flag flying here." If I ever hear that anthem, I am hurtled back to being seated around that large round teak table with its serviceable brown table cloth.

In the large dining extension, panelled in mahogany and with the French windows dressed with fashionable but serviceable velvet curtains in a shade that could only be described as startling tangerine, every small child was entitled to have their opinions heard whilst the adults listened.

Mother was a fervent educationalist and insisted all her grandchildren could read well by the age of four and were able to form a cogent argument by the time they were five years old.

It definitely worked because each small child hit the ground running when they started school and absorbed information like a sponge.

My father had been a trade union leader for a white collar union with all the immense power that that entailed in the 1970s. My mother had an intuitive grasp of labour history and economics and because of this had no time for the consecutive Conservative governments.

The Prime Minister, Margaret Thatcher in particular incurred her ire and she always known as TBW (That Bloody Woman) in our house. However, Mother mellowed in her personal opinion of Mrs Thatcher after reading a piece in the Guardian.

The story relayed the information with much detail. Apparently a young waitress had been serving prawn sandwiches to an assembled group at which Mrs Thatcher was present. The young woman had accidentally dropped the plate of sandwiches at the Prime Ministers feet. The article went on to explain that when the girl burst into tears, Mrs Thatcher did no more than drop to her knees and help her clear up the mess.

I was stunned when I heard Mother say "I think if you met her personally you would probably like her." However her opinion of the woman's politics changed not a jot until the day she died.

During those years of the seventies and eighties I would have loved to talk to my mother about marriage, childcare and life in general. However all she wanted to talk about the World politics, Idi Amin and Keynesian Economics. It was not that I did not care about these things, I really did, but I just wanted my mother to belong to me occasionally.

My mother had a beautiful face with stunning green eyes and since I was twelve I had been her honorary hair stylist, tasked with cutting, colouring and perming her hair.

In the early days when the fumes of whatever brand of perm we were using got too much for us in our tiny kitchen we would run outside giggling and gasping for air. I loved those occasional days of lightness and laughter.

My mother was slender and measured, steely and cool. She did not need to chat about inconsequential trivia; there was a world to put to rights and she was the woman to do it.

I was a grown up version of Millie Molly Mandy, rosy cheeked, always chatting and relentlessly cheerful. Every time I fell over I jumped right back up again and my indomitable spirit drove my poor mother mad. A childhood neighbour had once told me I was like one of those children's toys where you fill the bottom with sand and try to knock it down. The more you bashed it the faster it flew back up.

That same neighbour mentioned to my mother that she should think about entering me for the local Miss Whatever pageant, but this was absolutely against all Mother's ideals and as a consequence she never again paid much regard to Mrs Steel's prophecies again

Mrs Steel was convinced that women should not go to University because it put them off housework for life. She had the proof of this because her only treasured son Simon had married a very blasé pharmacist who at home did not pass muster.

Mother had just had her sixtieth birthday when our family moved south with Grant's new job. Even though I had seen her least once a month since we moved she no longer wanted any fuss and frippery. Her hair was now white as snow and she had it cut by a snippy woman called Julie, who professed to be a peripatetic hairdresser and came to the house once a month.

I do not know what Julie's job had been before her mobile career began but it certainly was not as a hairdresser. If she had used a bowl and knife and fork to cut it could not have looked worse. A jagged fringe and pair of clippers completed the uneven, urchin look.

I begged Mother to let me continue with her hair but she looked me sternly in the eye and said "Before I was sixty I did what other people wanted; now I have turned sixty and I am jolly well going to please myself"

I gave her a big hug and said if she changed her mind I would always be back up North in five hours.

Nobody ever saw mother's hair outdoors again however because when she went out as she took to wearing a pale grey beanie hat. Without lipstick and with an air of focused determination she became the bluestocking she had always dreamed of being.

Loving her as I did I just wish she had lived to see a New Labour government in power.

CHAPTER 99
A political change

An honest man in politics shines more than he would elsewhere.
Mark Twain

The Labour Party won the election in May 1997 after eighteen years of Tory rule and Tony Blair became Prime Minister. Good looking, young and a family man he appeared to be just what the country wanted. Those halcyon, sunny days of early May when he and his wife Cherie walked through the crowds shaking hands promised much, particularly for people on the centre left of politics.

One in four of the new MPs were women and that fact gladdened my heart. However the name "Blair's Babes" that was attached to the hundred and one Labour women Members of Parliament seemed fatuous to my ears.

This name was given after he was photographed standing, on the steps of Church House in Westminster surrounded by newly elected women in suits and high heels.

A lot of the women had stood for difficult seats and seemed a little shocked by winning and suddenly had to decide what to do about family responsibility. Of course they must have made plans but the reality was totally different.

No matter what a women's job entails, it is usually her that has to think about childcare, sports days, homework, difficult teenagers and diffident husbands.

No matter how many people a woman has to help her, I am afraid the buck always stops with her. It is you your baby wants, you your teenager blames and you that your husband misses.

The pervading atmosphere of change and hope lingered in the air for a while but I wondered how many of these intelligent and hard working women would stand again at the next election

Even though the all-women shortlist was used in the 2001 candidate selection procedure the number of women labour MPs went down to ninety seven. However this was in comparison to the number of women conservative MPs, which stood at only fourteen.

There was still much work to be done.

CHAPTER 100
The engagement in Paris

Grow old with me; the best is yet to be.
Robert Browning

When my daughter mentioned to me that she and her boyfriend Alistair were going to Paris for the weekend I did wonder to myself.

They were inveterate travellers and had visited most parts of the world but mostly as backpackers since leaving University. Paris would not have been their usual choice except for… could it possibly be an engagement?

They had been together for five years and seemed to have a lot of fun together. They had a stylish home in London and shared a haughty white Birmin cat called Django. They also had a large ginger moggy named Monty who condescended to live with them when he felt like eating the occasional meal. He was a farm cat and spent all day standing on the wall staring down at anybody that dared pass. He looked like Top Cat from the 1960s TV series and you half expected to see Officer Charlie Dibble wander up the road to chat to him.

The weekend of the Paris trip I waited with bated breath and sure enough when they came back happy and relaxed and announced that they were engaged.

Apparently Alistair had spoken to Grant to ask for his blessing two weeks before but my husband did say anything as he did want to spoil the surprise for me! Two things had been decided. Miranda was going to have a think about what kind of ring she wanted and the wedding was going to be the following year.

I was delighted as I really liked Alistair and thought they would be wonderful together. I said I was happy to be involved in the wedding preparations if they needed me. Lots of men are involved in their wedding plans now days but not so long ago fiancé involvement was frowned upon. All a man had to do was propose, buy the ring and turn up on the day.

Eventually Miranda asked one of Grant's cousin's husbands to make her ring as she wanted something unusual and stylish. He agreed and after a couple of meetings at his studio in London he came up with something amazing.

The unusual and contemporary ring really suits her and as the cousin has gone on has become one of the most famous jewellery designers in the world.

<h2 style="text-align:center">CHAPTER 101
Lilies and Mantovani</h2>

When you have two pennies left in the world, buy a loaf with one and a lily with the other.

Chinese Proverb

One day out of the blue my daughter rang me and said "I have two tickets for a wedding show in Kensington, do you fancy coming?" I agreed delightedly as honestly I would not have thought this was her kind of thing.

We arrived at the venue and as we walked in I was entranced by the scent of lilies and the Mantovani style serenades flowing out of every speaker. I looked at my daughter and she raised her eyebrows at me and I noticed her lips were set in a disapproving line

"Let's have a bit of lunch" she said and we walked across to the restaurant. When we were seated and waiting for our Caesar salads and chilled glasses of Vouvray she suddenly remarked "Gosh I like that".

I looked around to see a model sashaying down the runway in a black wedding dress followed by a dozen bridesmaids dressed in purple with black bouquets and gloves.

It was my turn to have the disapproving lips but then from somewhere came the words. "You must have what you want darling it's your day." We did not stay long but what happened next was one of the most embarrassing incidents I had ever endured.

When we left to walk to the tube station it was raining hard and the wind was blowing. We were glad we had brought scarves and turned our collars up against the squally conditions.

We scurried to the tube station, managed to scramble on to the next one and soon found ourselves at the mainline station. The platform was crowded and the wind was blowing a gale.

Miranda grabbed my arm to hurry me just as a gust of wind blew my large Mulberry scarf across my face. I did not want to lose it and so made a grab for it and threw it, as artfully as I could back over my shoulder.

I felt and then heard a delicate but very penetrating scream behind us that stopped us in our tracks. When I turned around there was a middle aged lady waving her arms in the air like a traffic policeman but the first thing I really noticed was her very strange hairstyle. It was very short and completely grey but her small head was covered in hundreds of Kirby grips all in close lines. I do not know if she was part of a silent order or whether the trauma of what had just happened to her had struck her dumb but she did not speak.

I realised that the poor woman was a nun just as Miranda said, "Oh my God mother, what have you done?", as she extracted the poor woman's head dress and wimple from inside my swaddled scarf.

It seems that as I had grabbed my scarf to stop it blowing away I had actually yanked the poor nun's wimple right off her poor head. I tried to help her put it back on but the scowling Mother Superior waved me away as I walked away backwards bowing as if I had just had an audience with the Queen.

I felt really terrible and wondered what the punishment was for disrobing a nun in public. Miranda and I waited arm in arm for the train not speaking even one single word to each other. About ten minutes passed before I dared look at her. I am ashamed to report we both giggled that much that we had to sit down.

The next two trains had passed before we recovered enough composure to resume our journey home.

CHAPTER 102
Do you remember where you were?

Being a princess is not all it's cracked up to be.
Princess Diana

There are certain events in life that stop you in your tracks and force you to remember exactly where you were at that precise moment.

The deaths of President Jack Kennedy and Beatle John Lennon are two such happenings that anchor that awful day forever in your memory bank.

The thirty first of August 1997 was one such day. It was the day Diana, Princess of Wales died in a car crash. It was early in the morning and we were lying in bed listening to Radio Four as we did every morning.

When the news of the tragedy came over the airways I jumped up and turned on the television that was in the corner of the bedroom. We really could not believe what we were seeing. It did not seem possible that such a vibrant, beautiful human being was gone forever.

Prince Charles and Princess Diana had been divorced the year before and were busy getting on with their own lives.

Princess Diana, who was the mother of the two Royal Princes, William and Harry, had been in Paris staying at The Ritz with her boyfriend Dodi Fayed after a holiday in the Riviera on a yacht.

The driver of the Mercedes, Henri Paul was killed as well as his passengers, Diana and Dodi in the crash at the Pont de L'Alma road tunnel. The only survivor was Trevor Rees Jones a body guard.

The paparazzi had been chasing the couple and photos of the terrible crash were on the television almost immediately.

Prince Charles and her sisters Lady Sarah McCorquodale and lady Jane Fellowes flew across to Paris to bring her body home.

The communal outpouring of grief that followed Diana's death was phenomenal and hardly believable. People were crying in the streets and over three million people onlookers and mourners lined the London streets.

The funeral was watched by two and a half billion people from over two hundred countries. The floral tributes around Kensington

Palace were in piles over five feet high and it seemed that nobody quite knew what to do with them.

I thought it was a dreadful family tragedy that such a young woman had been taken away from her precious sons but I wondered about the manifestation of the public outpouring of grief.

It seemed to me that Diana's life had been a catalyst for social change, with a more impassioned view of life, and her sudden and shocking death had become a metaphor for a lost age of innocence.

CHAPTER 103
The Prime Minister and the Queen

Life is just a journey.
Princess Diana

Diana's funeral was attended by many famous people from all walks of life including Elton John who sang his iconic version of *Candle in the Wind*.

The Royal Family like the rest of the country appeared not to know how to handle Diana's death. The Queen and the whole family were at their summer home at Balmoral and gave no indication of their feelings.

The population seemed not to understand the lack of emotion and the *Sun's* headline saying, "Where is our Queen?" chimed with popular feeling. There was also much dismay at their refusal to fly the royal flag at half mast.

The way that the Royal family insisted on observing protocol and the apparent lack of compassion did not endear them to the population. I thought it was just possible that they were busy consoling the important people, her two motherless sons.

Eventually the Queen came back to London and gave a speech to her people on September 9th. The new Prime Minister Tony Blair was credited with smoothing the path for a resolution of the public feelings.

Interest in Princess Diana seems to be unabated even as the years roll by.

She is buried on an island at her brother's home at The Althorpe Estate in Northamptonshire.

CHAPTER 104
Christmas lunch for twenty this year

May peace be your gift at Christmas and blessing all the year through.

Anonymous

Another Christmas rolled around and I started making plans. I had always loved Christmas and making my own mincemeat and Christmas cake was not a chore in any way. In fact with the radio on and a glass or two of sherry at your side it was just bliss.

I also dressed the house with holly, ivy and fresh green leaves from the garden. From being a bride of eighteen I had always planted hyacinths in white, blue and pink to decorate and perfume the house for the month of December. One of the first things I looked for in a new house was a dark corner to force hyacinth, daffodil and tulip bulbs for the home.

When we lived in the Lake District I bought mulberries by the sack full to freeze and then in September I would cover them with gin or even vodka to provide a warming nectar for our guests.

I always bought a large green ham weighing approximately twenty eight pounds every Christmas. Decades ago they were very salty and required a three day soak in the bath tub to remove the strong salt that they had been brined in.

A large ham caused my mother to nearly have heart failure one year when she was staying with us. I had placed the offending article in the bath long after she had gone to bed. My poor mother had got up in the night to spend a penny and as calm as her personality was she had let out a bloodcurdling scream that sent us all running!

I think I was always trying to recreate those perfect childhood Christmas times with my Grandmother Hester and her groaning dining room table and its delicious spread.

At Grandmother's there was always turkey, ham, cheese, salmon and handmade pork pies as well as salads of every description, However it was Grandmother Hester's puddings and deserts that were legendary in the family particularly anything to do with choux pastry.

Occasionally to everyone's amusement a delicate morsel might be dusted with a little ash because a Senior Service cigarette was never far from the corner of her mouth.

As well our nuclear family that year we had my sister Gillian, brother-in-law Malcolm and her children Claire and Rufus for the holidays. Two weeks before the date I spoke to my husband's sister Faith and she expressed a wish to come as well with her mother and teenage son. My sister Gillian and Grant's sister Faith had started school together when they were four years old and knew each other well. They did not see each other a lot but enjoyed catching up when they could.

We were twenty two that year for Christmas and I am so glad I had a chance for a last chat with my husband's mother.

My mother-in-law Laura had been a fixture in my life since I was a teenager. A wonderful mother to her four daughters she had absolutely no understanding of her only son. She had a miscarriage at forty eight years old and lost a little boy and for some reason that seemed to have coloured her relationship with her only son.

Grant was not close to her and whenever I suggested visiting his parents he just raised his eyebrows. Along with most women of my generation I was very respectful of my in laws and always made time for them.

Throughout my life I would never have dreamed of offering her a contrary opinion or a harsh word, it was just the way it was when I married her son and it was the way it continued all her life.

CHAPTER 105
Laura and her sisters

I don't need you to teach me how to handle my children, I live with one of yours and he definitely needs improvement.

Author unknown

Growing up as one of six sisters and widowed young, Laura was the matriarch of the family. In all the years I had known her we had never ever exchanged a comment about her son who also happened to be my husband. I suppose we were both too loyal to him.

However she had plenty of comments about my children who she thought I spoiled because they were always off skiing or horse riding or having fun.

However she had been a great support to me when I first went back to work and would travel the eighty miles on the bus to our house at a moment's notice. On the minus side she was critical and judgemental but on the plus side I knew she had a good heart underneath. She loved to play cards with children from when they were small because she said it helped them with their maths and always did my ironing rain or shine.

She spent the last years of her life living with her youngest daughter and grandson and had become rather crotchety in her late seventies.

Preparing Christmas for twenty two people for the holidays was tiring and although I loved the company I had foolishly left the wrapping of the presents until Christmas Eve.

I had asked for volunteers as I entered the crowded sitting room and those that did not ignore me shook their heads whilst failing to engage in eye contact.

Alone in our lilac and pale grey bedroom, I sat and stared at my reflection in the wardrobe mirrored doors. I thought to myself "Where do the years go?" but there was no answer available in the ether.

I was knee-deep in wrapping paper. I heard a shout from downstairs and realised it was my mother-in-law Laura leaning on her walker.

"I would really like to talk to you now" she said imperiously and beckoned me into the downstairs bathroom, which was set just by the front door.

I did as I was beckoned and went to settle her and began to look around the recently decorated room. This large room had remained the same for all the years we had lived in the house, with old fashioned blue tiles and striped 1980s wallpaper. As I looked around I felt a feeling of deep satisfaction at the new, soft cream Italian tiles and the modern square sinks where the taps turned themselves on and off again as if by magic.

"You were right you know." I looked around to see who had spoken. My biggest critic from my teens had said something nice to me? I turned to face her "About what Mother?" I said diffidently. "About everything I suppose" she replied.

The silence felt like a sticky, translucent cobweb between us. "I never knew him, he never spoke to me, and he was cleverer than the rest of us".

Her words became trapped and hung in the air. We stared at each other for a while and then I realised she was talking about her only son and my husband, Grant.

Lost in a reverie she continued "You were right about your children and their education as well. I am glad you did not listen to me".

I could not believe my ears and as I lifted her up and steadied her, she planted a kiss on my cheek, something she had never done in her life before. She leaned across the sink and lifted the pale cream Italian milled soap, washing her hands carefully as she stared into the mirror over the sink and then she sighed volubly.

I used a small brush to straighten her hair and handed her the emergency peach Max Factor lipstick from the cupboard under the sink.

Then with the water still running I thought I heard her say "Thank you for having us for Christmas"

"Oh it's been my pleasure," I gushed, "I have really enjoyed every minute of it and I hope you have too"

"You are a funny girl," she said staring at me.

Startled I asked, "Why ever would you say that?"

She replied in a firm voice "I actually said ….Thank you for helping me in the loo."

Satisfied she turned around, nodded and in one step of the walker we were plunged back into the melee.

CHAPTER 106
Are you a famous pop group?

Old age ain't no place for sissies.
Bette Davis

We all had a lovely Christmas and quiet New Year and then a few days later came the news that my mother-in-law Laura had fallen down the stairs and passed away. I was very sad but heartened by the conversation that we had been able to have a couple of weeks before then.

All the children decided to come to the funeral and they made arrangements to stay at a nearby hotel.

Grant and I arrived at his mother's home the morning of the funeral and as we walked in the sombre house Grant grabbed my hand and whispered "Oh Please, please I cannot go in".

"Whatever is the matter love," I said as I turned to face him. Ashen, he was staring through in to conservatory.

"Oh God, she is there lying on the dining table" he whispered in a strangled voice.

I looked up and permitted myself a smile.

The long dining room table had been laid for the reception and the food covered with a long pink table cloth. I walked through and lifted the corner of the cloth and as Grant nearly passed out, he realised he was looking at a large salad bowl.

The children arrived not long afterwards. Our children and their partners were all tall and broad, dressed in formal dark business suits. However I could tell they had all been laughing.

"Whatever is it?" I whispered.

"The taxi driver has just asked us if we are a famous pop group and we had to tell the poor man we were going to our Grandmother's funeral. He was so embarrassed" said my daughter and then her face fell as she looked towards her sad aunts.

She had always been fond of her paternal grandmother and the news of her demise had hit her hard.

Lots of Grant's childhood friends were at the church and I looked around at these men I had known from boyhood. I wondered then why it is some people manage to stay the same and others looked entirely different as they enter middle age.

As we sat around talking in a desultory manner after the service I wondered about my youngest sister-in-law Faith and how she would manage without her mother in her life. I hoped that she would find some freedom and contentment as I knew the previous years had been extremely hard on her.

We drove back south the following day and I asked Grant how he felt about losing his mother. "I feel nothing really but I know life must go on" was his reluctant reply.

A tiny thought fleetingly scattered across my mind at that point. I remembered a motherly beauty therapist that had once said something to me while she was doing my nails.

As I looked at her she bit her bottom lip for a moment, "I have told all my girls; never marry a man who does not like his mother because, sure as eggs are eggs, you are going to turn into her one day".

I laughed at the time but when I thought about it, a little frisson of fear fluttered across my heart as I stared out onto the open road.

CHAPTER 107
Finding the right outfit

Fashion fades only style remains the same.
Coco Chanel

Week after week some kind friend or family member accompanied me on a shopping trip to find a suitable outfit for my daughter's wedding.

I had the colour in mind but could not see the ideal design in my head. Being a visual person meant I always knew what I wanted before I set out shopping, but this time my mind was absolutely full with wedding preparations.

Of course my real self-inflicted problem was that I was two sizes bigger than I had been three years before at my oldest son's wedding. I had many excuses for this increased girth including giving up my job, my ill health and not living so near to the gym.

However, when I really thought about it though, there was only one culprit. My perfect passion for the ancient art of home baking was my definite downfall. A batch of sultana scones with homemade blackberry jam, a quick coffee and walnut cake, a delicious cherry clafoutis or windfall apple pie appeared daily on the kitchen counter in our house as if by some magical force.

Now, some people can bake and then will derive a vicarious pleasure from just watching their guests consume the tasty morsels they had just been prepared.

However, I believed politeness in company meant sharing and that included the pleasure of me eating as well.

I was actually quite prepared for all this sharing, as in my tea time cupboard resided Grandmother Alexandra's antique faded pink and green rose cake plates with a matching three tier cake stand.

Where these had come from I had no idea as I am convinced that my grandmother had never ever made a cake in her life. She had been too busy living her life outside the home to "faff around in the kitchen" as she referred to cooking,

I also possessed six dainty silver hallmarked forks that I had bought from The Lanes, in Brighton about twenty five years before. I loved silver but the chore of polishing it was sometimes beyond me.

Although I had plenty of practice of polishing silverware as a child, because so many of my relatives had owned hotels.

My tea cups and saucers were of a blue Wedgewood design and had a china and silver cake server to match. My colleagues at work had bought these lovely things for me when I left my job in East Anglia.

Also in the tea time cupboard was an ornate Capo de Monte tray that had belonged to a Great Aunt Ethel. I also was the proud owner of an exquisite white handmade lace tray cloth that had been a gift from a friend whilst we were on a business trip in the Alps. I loved just running my hand along its delicate scalloped edges as it immediately took me back to the picturesque village of Gstaad.

For a few months I had also been the recipient of Grandmother Hester's silver tray and matching teapot, milk jug and sugar bowl. This collection had caused much heated discussion in the extended family as it had once belonged to Great Grandmother Hannah and then Grandmother Hester, before arriving ceremoniously in my mother's utilitarian wooden sideboard.

As nothing of Mother's slender jewellery fitted me, my father had suggested I have the family silver service. One day, not long after Mother died, my sister had Gillian admired it. I gave it to her right there and then as she so rarely remarked on possessions and it was lovely to see her smile.

They only bought two albums that year. I bought "*Quench*" by the Beautiful South. I loved all their songs but thought the words of Perfect 10 were funny and inclusive. I still have that song on my phone.

I also bought "*Believe*" by Cher which was the biggest selling song of the year. I admired her spirit and determined attitude. My list of women I admired started with people like Maya Angelou and Hilary Clinton but included Cher as well. Her beauty, energy and youthfulness empowered me and others like me to believe we could do it, whatever it was.

Her age seemed to have no effect whatsoever on her spirit or beauty and that's how it must be as we face the future.

CHAPTER 108
The baking paraphernalia

Find something you're passionate about and keep tremendously interested in it.

Julia Child

In fact I had all my mother's baking paraphernalia as nobody else wanted any of it. Mother possessed jelly moulds, china baking beans, cake tins, copper pate moulds, biscuit cutters, spoons, baking weights and many more things I found at the back of the cupboard and I could only guess what they were originally meant to accomplish. There is still a roll of stiff, crackled grease proof paper from the year 1962 in my baking cupboard. I also have a jar of ancient dried butter beans that I remember my mother using when I was a child to stop the pastry crust for the delicate egg custard rising.

Of all my mother's baked delicacies, egg custard was the family favourite. With its gently wobbling top and vanilla scented, creamy interior it tasted like the food of the gods.

I also had all her cookery books and elegant hand written recipes. I could only look at her cooking missives occasionally though as her beautiful, neat handwriting broke my heart, in a way that her photograph or a recording of her mellifluous voice never could.

Mother was a fan of popular cooks of the day Marguerite Patton and later Mary Berry. She found both their styles very plain and no nonsense, which she admired enormously. She found Fanny Craddock far too showy and would turn off the television with a "Tut" if she appeared.

Mother had wonderful hands for short crust and puff pastry; always cool with elegant, long, fluttering fingers.

However I had perfect hands for bread making, capable and wide with strong fingers and with a capacity to keep going at all cost.

This made me a perfect candidate for choux pastry and that was the secret of my baking success.

I had always bought puff pastry, as I heartily agreed with Grandmother Alexandra about all that faffing about being a waste of time. I could produce very passable short crust pastry with the judicious use of very cold water and a special flat knife to mix it all together. Then I always ran my hands under the cold water tap before I commenced the very fast and feather light pressure task of the rolling out procedure.

My skill with choux pastry involved boiling water, butter and a little sugar and salt together, then flinging flour at the resultant liquid very fast and always in one go. Then quickly one has to set about beating it with a large wooden spoon until the ball leaves the sides of the pan.

Whilst I waited for it to cool I mixed together six egg yolks and then added them slowly one by one.

This is where I excelled as I could keep beating ferociously until suddenly the yellowy, glossy gloop became a thing of shining intensity. A very hot oven would complete the magic show.

Choux pastry is a phenomenon of chemistry that means mere mortals can transform every day ingredients such as eggs, flour and butter into ambrosia. These were turned into exquisite tiny chocolate éclairs, huge cream coffee puffs, Religieuse, Paris Brest and the thing my children loved the most when they were small, delicate, perfectly shaped swans.

My repertoire also included myriad puff pastry deserts. These including tarte tatin, buttery, sugar laden currant Eccles cakes, apple strudel that improved with a chunk of Wensleydale cheese and the famous strawberry cream millefiulle which graced special occasions the length and breadth of the land.

My reputation for being able to whip up a batch of fruit scones in the time it took to make a pot of earl grey tea was not exaggerated and much tested.

Bread dough was made into glistening Chelsea buns, banana bread and maple date nut bread just to mention a few sticky delicious delights.

Sugar coated puff pastry Palmiers and chocolate peanut biscuits never made it from the cooling rack to the plate in our house.

Strong hands also made for perfect hot water crust for game pie and my husband's favourite, pork pies for high days and holidays.

My cakes tended to include something healthy so carrot cake also contained courgettes grown in profusion by the back door. The flowers stuffed with ricotta cheese for a tasty treat.

Fruit cakes contained just about everything including dates, raisins, apricots and currants all chopped up small and my coffee and walnut cake was sold at fetes all over the Lake District.

Of course all this arm aching effort can now be replaced by the precious pink Kitchen Aid fairy that sits proudly on the black granite surface and this machine can do just about everything except serve lunch.

This treasured birthday present managed to equip me with the one cookery skill I could never master. My Meringues and Pavlovas have journeyed through space and time from flat, watery pools to scrumptious, billowy, clouds that entrance everybody who gets a serving including me.

The discovery, that my strenuous efforts at making perfect Pavlovas were forever doomed in the humid and rainy conditions that existed in Manchester, North Wales and the Lake District where I lived for years, had set me free.

On one rainy, lazy Saturday afternoon I had been watching *Gone with the Wind* and Rhett Butler had just said " Frankly my dear, I don't give a damn"… and I thought " Hmm, that's my cue to put the kettle on."

As I leaned over I happened to press the remote control with my bottom and of its own accord it changed the station over to the cookery channel.

This was just in time for the cheery presenter, who I did not recognise, to inform me that "Meringues hate damp weather".

"Ah ha!" was all I could think of to say as I struggled to my feet.

In the three months before my daughter's wedding I walked every single day rain or shine and was always very careful to abstain from anything that was neither fish nor salad.

The pale blue Paule Vasseur outfit I eventually bought was gorgeous and in the end only one fitting larger than my normal size.

However, in my own mind whenever I look at the picture of me from that day the only thing I can find to admire about myself is my well- turned ankle.

CHAPTER 109
The night before the Wedding

Love conquers all things except poverty and toothache.
Mae West

The men in the family all left the house the evening before the wedding and bridesmaids started to arrive from about four pm. There was a general air of fun and excitement and as we were all sitting in the kitchen one of them said "Where's the bride?"

We went round the long kitchen pine table and one by one they shook their heads. There was a lot of "I thought she was with you" going on but eventually we realised nobody had any idea where the expected belle of the ball could be.

Like her maternal grandmother Mona my daughter was never one for fuss or frippery so most of the plans for the wedding had been made with her endorsement but not much of her input.

At six pm with the brides and bridesmaids dresses hanging from every available surface, I was beginning to feel my concern rise up a notch to mild panic. Then thankfully I recognised her car lights coming down the drive.

As I opened the front door I had to smile. She had scores of tiny yellow rollers in her long auburn hair.

She smiled, kissed my cheek and proceeded to unpack Chinese food for twenty people out of the boot of her car. She had been sitting in the hairdressers for four hours.

The bridesmaids were all having their hair up in a chignon tomorrow and we needed to fix three hundred tiny pink roses to hair clips by morning so the hairdressers could weave them in and out. I took out my mother's sewing box and handed needles round the table.

The older girls had a glass of chilled Chablis and the younger ones had apple juice as we sat around the table sewing and talking.

A little while later I realised that there was a lot of laughter going on around the room.

"Okay, own up." I said, "What is happening?"

It seemed that I had been sewing roses on the requisite hair clips without my glasses on. Every time I had attached one and laid it on the table, the person sitting next to me had handed it on to another person to re-stitch.

The girls all thought it was hilarious so I went into the den to watch the news whilst they calmed down. I took a small glass of brandy with me to steady my nerves.

Lots of noise and rising merriment was going on as the younger bridesmaids were heading up to bed and so I administered a hot chocolate with marshmallows to anybody who wanted one. The stirring and sipping seemed to calm them and they were all fast asleep as their heads hit the pillow.

The older girls stayed up for hours catching up and because we had so many guests that night my daughter and I were sharing a room, which actually worked out perfectly.

We had a little problem because her cream cashmere v neck sweater would not go over her head because of the rollers. In the end with much discussion and laughter we had to cut it down the front to get it over her head.

We chatted long into the night about what being married would mean to her life. I also told her about my wedding day exactly thirty years before hers and we giggled about some of the fashions of the day.

Eventually we settled and she fell asleep wondering how she could feign a look of surprise when being finally told of her honeymoon destination of the Maldives as she had already found the tickets on the kitchen table!

CHAPTER 110
The morning of the Wedding

Today is the first day of the rest of your life.
Anonymous

We were all up early and croissants demolished before taxis arrived to take the bride and bridesmaids to the hairdressers. I waited at home for the flowers to arrive and allowed myself a small glass of sherry whilst listening to John Peel's *Home Truths* on Radio Four

The programme had begun a few months ago and I had become addicted to his easy listening presenting style. I loved his voice from his Radio One days but this was something else. There were no celebrities' stories just "ordinary" people and their fascinating lives.

This programme and *Letter from America* by Alistair Cooke were two weekend treats not to be missed in our house.

Just as I looked around and distractedly glanced at my watch, Heather the florist, in her green and white van of delight arrived on the drive. Millie the Saturday girl and Heather jumped out and between the three of us the dining room and kitchen were soon full of perfectly formed flowers. Heather had decorated the Norman church in the village the night before but still had to put out the decoration for the lych-gate and church foyer so she was quickly on her way.

As I opened the first cream box and moved the tissue aside the exquisite perfume filled the house. I carefully took out Miranda's bouquet which was an exact replica of her Grandmothers 1940s Arum Lily, White Peony and asparagus fern confection that nearly reached to the floor. I held it to my heart for a moment and thought about my mother and how she would have loved this day.

The four older bridesmaid's bouquets came next. They were wearing deep pink and their bouquets of cream lilies were a perfect complement to the dresses. The four younger bridesmaids were wearing the palest of cream and they carried tiny posies of pink sweet peas and white freesias. The perfume from them was divine.

I suddenly realised that the stamens from the Lilies were still in place and so I took them through to the laundry and used the kitchen scissors to remove every trace. The last thing we wanted was yellow pollen over everybody.

Once I was satisfied everything was in order I stood in the hall and looking round said to myself "How wonderful, I am going to enjoy this day."

I arrived at the hairdressers at the same time as Grant as he was picking up the smaller bridesmaids. We exchanged a rueful smile as the rain had just started to fall.

Simon, my hairdresser asked me if I was fine as he began to work his magic on my hair. The lady who usually brought me coffee arrived with a glass of champagne. I looked across at my daughter who was still in the midst of having her hair put up in an intricate style and she winked at me.

She was right as the champagne bubbles calmed my nerves.

Simon began to put my hair up in a chignon and when it was finished and, lacquered for a hurricane, he added my blue silk pearl fascinator.

Eventually we were all ready and arrived back in the house in plenty of time. I had left a lunch spread of various salads and a chicken chasseur in the slow cooker on the table in the conservatory. There seemed to be scores of people milling around the house, eating lunch and chatting about the weather.

Eventually after much hinting and then a definite shooing away the only people that were left were the bride, her parents and her bridesmaids. The photographer had been there for some time and he eventually wanted the bridesmaids for a photograph in the garden under the apple trees. Fortunately the clouds had gone away and the mellow October sun was beginning to both warm and delight us.

I marvelled at the show the garden put on at this time of year with the autumn colours of the dahlias and chrysanthemums. These colours were offset by the sparkling white of the last hurrah of the ubiquitous cosmos, which grew around the garden with abandon.

As the bridesmaids, ranging in age from five to twenty five, stood waiting for a photograph, I could see how nervous they all were. I ran back into the kitchen for the Bach Flower Remedy and went along the row dispensing a few drops under each girl's tongue. They were chattering and giggling and each one looked like a princess in her wonderful gown.

The two ancient white cars arrived to take them and very soon they were off to the church. When I went back in to the house I could see my husband Grant in his morning suit looking out at the autumn garden with his hands behind his back. Lost in his own thoughts I imagined that he was feeling a little nervous and sentimental.

I ran upstairs to my daughter's bedroom to make sure she was ready. I stopped, gasping at her beauty and radiance and then followed her carefully back down the winding staircase. Her shantung silk dress of the palest cream had a long train and the bodice was exquisitely embroidered with tiny flowers and seed pearls. She looked so beautiful that neither of us could speak and tearfully we both rushed forward to hug her at the same time.

Just then my car arrived and just as I was getting into it, the open topped vintage Rolls Royce arrived for the bride and her father. I blew them a kiss and set off for my journey to the church.

I must admit to feeling a little lonely on the fifteen minute journey to the village church as both our sons were already at the church, acting as ushers for the congregation.

As I arrived in the foyer I took a deep breath, smiled at the bridesmaids and began the walk into the church where hundreds of our nearest and dearest where waiting. The guests had come from all over the world and it was heart-warming to see everybody in their finery looking so happy.

I looked across at the groom Alistair and his best man, then the organist began George Frederic Handel's "*Arrival of the Queen of Sheba*" and the whole congregation rose to its feet as one with a sigh of anticipation, as if they were a single entity.

The Bride and her Father arrived at the church door and they began their procession down the aisle. When they arrived at the altar the couple smiled at each other and then the long silk train of Miranda's dress rustled as she turned to give her maid of honour and oldest cousin Claire, her Arum Lily bouquet. I caught her eye and thought my daughter looked so beautiful, calm and reassured.

My husband came back to stand by my side and the service began. The smaller bridesmaids took their seats and I checked that the older girls were feeling fine as they stood behind the bride and groom in the aisle.

Then I looked down at the order of service to see which hymn would come first, because I knew the couple had chosen their hymns from a selection of those that had been composed by one of the groom's great grandfathers.

I smiled to myself as the whole congregation once more rose to their feet with one single movement and began to sing that most famous of hymns *"Fight the Good Fight"* to the tune of Pentecost.

* * *

THE END

Recipes from our travels

Number One:-   **Strawberry Millefeuille**

Go out and buy a packet of puff pastry! Put the oven onto a high temperature. Roll out and cut pastry into three rectangles and place on greased baking sheets. Place into a hot oven and leave for twenty minutes until well risen. Whip cream until thick and keep in fridge until needed. Mix icing sugar with water and keep a tablespoon of icing on one side. Put in fridge. Take strawberries, hull and cut in half adding a tiny amount of icing sugar and a squeeze of lemon. When the pastry is fully cold lay the first rectangle on plate. Spoon on a tablespoon of good strawberry jam and add half the cream, followed by half the strawberries. Repeat the process until you have added the last pastry rectangle. Pour on cool, thick icing and spread it out.

Pop the millefeuille back in fridge and add a few grains of instant coffee let down with a drop boiling water to the last spoon of icing. Take out desert and draw two equally spaced coffee lines down the icing. Use a skewer draw lines back and forward across the icing to make a feathered pattern.

This is a fabulous dish for a party and keeps well overnight in the fridge.

The most I have ever made in one time is twenty for a large engagement party and every morsel disappeared!

Number Two:- **Pork and Mushrooms in Marsala Wine**
Cream Sauce

A pork fillet will feed four people. Double all quantities if you need more.

Slice one pork fillet crossways into pieces about half an inch thick. Bash them lightly with a rolling pin and dust lightly with flour, cover and refrigerate. Slice a small onion, clove of garlic and as many mushrooms as you like.

Fry the onions in a little olive oil, add the garlic and mushrooms and when everything looks done add a little white wine, tablespoon of Dijon mustard, table spoon of honey, chicken stock, tarragon or rosemary and salt and pepper. Simmer for a minute before adding double cream. In another pan fry the pork roundels for a minute neither on each side being sure nor to crowd the pan. When all the pork is cooked, pour in a shot of Marsala wine or brandy to deglaze the pan then pour the sauce contents over the meat and bubble for a moment until piping hot. This whole dish can be cooked in ten minutes and with Marsala wine and cream is ambrosia.

Of course a plainer version without alcohol and double cream tastes good as well. To bring creaminess to the dish add two tablespoonful's of 0% fat Greek yoghurt at the end; just remember not to boil the dish after you have added it. I serve this with mashed potatoes to soak up the delicious sauce and a mix of steamed broccoli and asparagus spears.

Number Three:-   **Grandmothers Raspberry Trifle**

You will need an old fashioned glass bowl to serve this in. I buy mine in charity shops when I see them in the window and now have quite an eclectic collection going back to the 1930s.

Ingredients: Raspberry Jelly, Raspberry Blancmange, 3 tablespoons of castor sugar. 1 pint of full cream milk. A large carton of Double Cream. Fresh, Frozen or tinned Raspberries. Cassis or Raspberry cordial. Flaked Almonds. Make the jelly according to instructions and when cool add raspberries and cassis or cordial. Put the jelly in fridge to set.

Make a pink blamange with pint of milk or you could use custard if you prefer. When the blamange is hot put it in a jug and sprinkle the top with a spoon of sugar to stop a skin forming. When it is cool pour onto the custard and put back in the fridge.

Whip the double cream until billowy and add sugar to taste. Spread over blamange. Toast almonds carefully in a small pan and when cool sprinkle on top. Leave a couple of hours before serving.

The alternative to this dish is to add bananas and sprinkle chocolate on top. Delicious served either way.

Number Four:-   **My Simnel Cake**

Four large eggs,250g each butter, brown sugar and self-raising flour.750g total of a mix of sultanas, glace cherries, currants, chopped dried figs .The grated rind of 2 lemons and I orange and 1tsp mixed spice. Tablespoon of ground almonds. 2 readymade packets of marzipan weighing 500 g each. 7 inch cake tin and oven at 150 degrees.

Pre-heat a cool oven for ten minutes.Put butter and sugar into bowl. Beat them until pale then add the beaten eggs, flour and mixed spice alternately. Stir in the zest and chopped dried fruit and mix well. Put half of cake mixture in a floured and lined tin. Chop one block of marzipan in equal small pieces and spread equally over the top. Cover with the rest of the cake mix and put it in the oven about 3 hours, but test with a skewer after 2 hours and when it comes out clean the cake is ready. When the cake is cool, turn it over so the flat surface is at the top. Use the remaining block of marzipan to decorate the top. The ground almonds make it easier to roll. The traditional decoration is to roll the marzipan flat, cut into strips and then criss cross them in a basket weave pattern across the top. If you like you can put it under the grill to brown slightly. If there is any marzipan left you can save it to decorate homemade hot cross buns.

Number Five:-   **Our House Chicken Chasseur**.

2 chicken thighs per person. Chopped bacon, mushrooms, shallots or red onion and garlic. Olive oil, butter, glass of red wine, tomato puree, red pepper paste, a splash of Worcester sauce ,dried herbs,(Thyme or oregano) salt and pepper. Chicken stock to cover. Fresh herbs to garnish.

Melt butter in oil in frying pan then add seasoned chicken. Fry for about 5 minutes turning until brown then take out of pan and keep warm. Fry the onions, garlic, bacon and mushrooms for a few minutes until cooked then add the red wine to deglaze pan.

Add stock and whatever you have of the other ingredients. Bubble sauce for a few minutes, put the chicken back in and cook for about 45 minutes in a medium oven with a lid on. Remove the chicken, bubble the sauce hard to reduce it then replace the chicken, stir and garnish with parsley or whatever you have on the window ledge. This is delicious with roast potatoes that can go in the oven at the same time as the chicken.

Number Six **My Quick Beef Bourgogne.**

Two large steaks either rib eye, sirloin or rump. Sliced mushrooms chopped shallots, spring onions or red onion and garlic. A mix of vegetable stock, red wine, mustard, soy sauce, honey, tomato puree, red pepper paste, paprika, salt and black pepper. Any dried and fresh herbs. I use dried oregano and fresh parsley but others will suffice.

This is my favourite dish when two nice steaks have to feed four people in a hurry. Slice the steaks in narrow strips across the grain making them into bite size pieces. Heat olive oil in frying pan and when it is hot add the steak strips. Cook on one side and flip them over. The whole process should take about three minutes. Remove and keep warm.

Add a little more oil to pan and add chopped onions and mushrooms plus a little garlic. Stir and cook until brown then add the wine to deglaze the pan. Cook for a minute then add the stock and whatever mix of mustard, soy sauce, honey, tomato puree, pepper paste, paprika, salt and pepper suits your taste. Stir and bubble for a couple of minutes and then add the steak and juices back to the pan. Another minute of stirring provides a heavenly dish in ten minutes flat. Serve with a green salad and crusty bread or good quality readymade mash.

THE END

9 781909 421516